Fairfax County, Virginia

Will Book Abstracts

1767–1783

Ruth and Sam Sparacio

Heritage Books
2023

HERITAGE BOOKS
AN IMPRINT OF HERITAGE BOOKS, INC.

Books, CDs, and more—Worldwide

For our listing of thousands of titles see our website
at
www.HeritageBooks.com

Published 2023 by
HERITAGE BOOKS, INC.
Publishing Division
5810 Ruatan Street
Berwyn Heights, MD 20740

International Standard Book Number
Paperbound: 978-1-68034-549-0

FAIRFAX COUNTY, VIRGINIA

WILL BOOK C
20 May 1767 - 16 December 1776

pp. Appraisal of the Estate of GEORGE JOHNSTON Esqr. taken this 11th
1- day of February 1767 .. items valued and totalled, £ 1554.10.3 ..
6 made by appraisers John West, John Carlyle, John Dalton.

At a court held .. xxth May 1767 .. inventory was returned and ordered to be recorded.

pp. The whole amount of the Sale of the Estate of DANIEL JENNINGS,
6- deced, & to whom sold .. purchasers .. Thomas Awbrey, James Robertson,
7 Ben. Sebastian, John Watson, William Boylstone, Joseph Earp, John Hunter, Townshend Dade, James Leith, John Templeman, Gerrard Trammell, William Guy, Benjamin Diamond, Henry Garrett, James Hamilton, William Saunders, John Brawner, William Hardin, James Scott, Joseph Allan, William Shortridge, Jeremiah Hampton, John Hurst, James Green, John Rattcliff, William Gray, Thomas Power, Thomas Ford, John Ford, Peter Turley, George Landman, Sampson Demovil, Mr. Gerrard Alexander, Daniel Jennings, James Jennings .. value of sale £ 189.14.9 .. true account by Benj. Sebastian, sold for Mr. Gerrd. Alexander, Executor.

At a court held 19th May 1767 .. this account of Sale returned and ordered to be recorded.

pp. Will of HUGH WEST. I HUGH WEST of county of Fairfax .. Attorney
7- at Law .. do on this 30th day of March 1767 .. desire my body be de-
8 cently interred at the direction of my beloved wife, ELIZABETH WEST, & my Brothers, JOHN WEST, GEORGE WEST & WILLIAM WEST, whom I appoint Executors .. I desire that all my just debts be paid And in order to Enable my Executors to do so I hereby order that they .. do sell & dispose of my whole Estate (my dwelling Plantation & adjacent lands excepted) .. Whereas I have agreed with Mr. BRYAN FAIRFAX for certain lands adjoining my dwelling plantation & have already paid him in part the sum of Ninety Eight pounds current money, it is my will my Executors, after discharging my debts, pay Mr. Fairfax the money that shall remain in their hands & take his deed in the name of my children .. but if my Executors shall think it more to the advantage of my children to have no more land from Mr. Fairfax than I have already paid for, my desire is that they then apply the Overplus as my Executors shall think proper. As to the land whereon I live & which is before excepted from the Sale of my other lands, I desire it may be equally divided in Quantity & Quality, if my wife should now be with child & have a son, I desire my son have his choice of one moiety .. the other moiety to be equally divided among my three daughters, SYBIL, JEMIMA & SARAH, but if my wife should bear a girl, then my desire is that the whole tract of land be equally divided among my four daughters as coheirs .. My will that my Executors shall not find it necessary to sell my lands already mentioned to be sold, that then the said land be equally divided among all my children born or unborn. My will that my right to the Lotts in the Town of Alexandria be sold by my Executors when they shall think it fit together with the Reversion. Whereas I am entitled to a proportion of my Father's personal estate after the decease of my Mother, my will that my beloved wife have her dower in the said part on my Mother's decease, that the remainder descend to my children. My will my wife have the sold Guardianship of my children during the term of her widowhood but if she should intermarry again, then it is my will

that my Brothers, JOHN, GEORGE & WILLIAM, do take upon them the guardianship ;.

Presence: Sarah Manley, H. West
S. West, Wm. Rumney, Jam. Colquhorn,
Wm. Triplett.

At a court held .. 18th June 1767 .. will presented by ELIZABETH WEST, JOHN WEST & GEORGE WEST .. proved by oath of SYBIL WEST & WILLIAM RUMNEY .. and at a court held .. xxth July in the year aforesaid WILLIAM WEST, Clerk, made oath hereto & was further proved by oath of WM. TRIPLETT & ordered to be recorded.

p. 9 1767. Estate of FUTERAL HALL, decd, to ANN HALL. By sale of whole Estate amount'g to £ 42.17.5; by Tobacco rated in money 2428. ANN HALL, Administratrix.

At a court held .. 19th August 1767 .. ANN HALL, administratrix of FUTERAL HALL, decd .. being examined by the Court is allowed & ordered to be recorded.

pp. 9-10 Will of ALEXANDER MILLS. I ALEXANDER MILLS of County of Fairfax .. give to my son, GEORGE MILLS, all my wearing Cloaths except one Sagathy Coat, also one brindle cow & four dollars Cash. I give to my youngest daughter, REBECCA MILLS, 990 pounds of crop tobacco & Cash towards maintaining her or for them to receive the said Tobacco who has the child, REBECCA, after my will is in force .. I give to my youngest son, ALEXANDER MILLS, my land whereon I now live containing 123 acres .. if he dies without heirs .. land should fall to my son, JOHN MILLS .. furthermore it is my desire said land be for use & service of all my children, Vizt. ANN MILLS, JNO. MILLS, MARY MILLS, ELIZABETH MILLS & REBECCA MILLS .. my desire that my five children have two years schooling a piece out of my Estate. All the rest of my Estate to be Equally divided among my six children (ALEXANDER MILLS listed with others named above) .. appoint my son in law, THOMAS PERKINS & my Eldest daughter, ANN MILLS, to be my Executors .. this 27th day of June 1767.

Presence: Elijah Williams, Alexr. x Mills
Joseph Jacobs, Mordecai x Jacobs

At a court held .. 16th November 1767 .. will presented by THOMAS PERKINS & ANN MILLS .. proved by oaths of JOSEPH JACOBS & MORDECAI JACOBS .. is admitted to record .. certificate is granted (Executors) for obtaining a probate thereof in due form.

pp. 10-13 Inventory of Mr. HUGH WEST'S Estate, Augt. 28, 1767 .. items valued but not totalled .. made by appraisers CHA. BROADWATER, HENRY GUNNELL, BENJA. MOODY.

At a court held .. 17th Novr. 1767 .. inventory returned and ordered to be recorded.

pp. 13-14 1765. ANNE & URSELEY SPENCE in account with DANIEL NEAL .. some entries .. to JEMIMAH GUNNELL for making three suits negroe Cloaths .. ferriage of two negroes over Occoquan .. my trouble going up to Fairfax selling the Estate, hiring the negroes, 27 days .. cash paid Mr. DAVID BOYD, Lawr. .. paid SHAPLEY NEALL .. paid Capt. JOHN DALTON; paid Shapley Neal for bring ANNE SPENCE down; paid Mr. WILLIAM PIERCE for schooling URSELEY SPENCE; paid Mr. JOHN BALLANDINE JUNR.; boarding & mending & making for ANNE & URSLEY SPENCE 1 year; paid Mr. WILLIAM ELLZEY: paid for MAJ. WAGGONER for Inverty of Estate; paid RICHARD

NEALE for bringing URSLEY SPENCE down; balance due orphans 2.6.1 .. Contra. .. by cash of JEMIMAH WEST; THOMAS MONROE; JOHN POSEY; JOHN YEOMAN; SHAPLEY NEALL; Mr. THOMAS SHAW .. balance at £ 43.5.0.

At a court held .. 18th Novr. 1767 .. DANIEL NEALE, guardian of ANN SPENCE & URSULA SPENCE exhibited this account .. same being examined by the court is allowed and ordered to be recorded.

pp. 14-16 DR. LAWRENCE WASHINGTON, decd, Estate account continued .. 1756 Dec. 17 cash paid COLL. GEORGE LEE; to Mr. GEDNEY CLARKE; to STEPHEN LEWIS; to Hunting Creek Inspectors; to your subscription for the courthouse; to WILLIAM WAITE; to JOHN SHERADINE share of crop; to JOHN HEARTLEY do .. (1758) to JACOB ROGERS; RICHARD HALBERT; Mr. ROBT. JACKSON; To 8 Motto rings lost by Capt. Lee; (1759) to ALLEN MACRAY for a velvet cap for Miss W. .. (1760) to WM. ROSS; Mr. GEORGE JOHNSTON'S lawyer; to GERSHAM KEYS; to GEORGE MASON Esqr. paid JAMES MERCER; to ROBT. ADAM'S Sheriff's fees; to DANIEL LAWRENCES notes now in court; to THOMAS CRAWFORD; balance due from JOHN CARLYLE. CONTRA. (1756). GERSHAM KEYS per judgment (186.12.6); (1757) Sundrie sums recd MICHL. MELTON, SOLOMON NICHOLS, COLE GRAYSON, HENRY BIGGS, RD. STEPHENS, RICHARD MORGAN; cash of CHRISTOPHER HARDWICK for corn; of GEORGE MUL for rent of Lotts; DANIEL LAWRENCE rent of lots; JOHN HEARTLEY for sundries in Frederick; JOHN PATTINSON for Lotts & Int. Balance at 427.10.2½.

At a court held .. 23rd March 1768 .. JOHN CARLYLE one of the Executors of LAWRENCE WASHINGTON Esqr., decd, exhibited this account and same being examined by the court is allowed and ordered to be recorded.

pp. 16-17 DR. LAWRENCE WASHINGTON, decd, Estate Account. (1755) cash to JNO. ORR for Mr. BEVENS bill & protest & charges; paid Dockr. FLOOD; Capt. McCARTY'S Exrs.; WILLIAM BLACK; JAMES HOAR; NATH. CHAPMAN.

CONTRA. my bill on Sir N. CAREW & COMPANY; JOHN STORK: cash Coll. LOMAX .. Balance at Tobo 8826 £ 920.0.6. Errors Excepted Augt 6th 1757, AUGUSTINE WASHINGTON.

At a court held .. 23rd March 1768 .. on motion of JOHN CARLYLE, Gent., this account is ordered to be recorded.

pp. 17-19 DR. Estate of SAMUEL CANTERBURY, decd .. 1764. Paid Mr. ALEXR. HENDERSON; paid Revd. Mr. GREEN for sermon; paid WILLIAM BARKER; SARAH SMITH a midwife; THOMAS WINDSOR; SARAH WINDSOR; DAVID HUGHES; BENJAMIN SEBASTIAN; Capt. G. JOHNSTON; CHARLES CORNISH; JOSEPH STEVENS per order of Court; Doct. JAM. LAURIE; JAMES ALLEN; JOHN MINOR for taxes; JOHN BRYAN a legacy; LEWIS RENO; MOSES SIMPSON; RICHD. SIMPSON; THOMAS LAWSON; GEO. SIMPSON; JOHN RILEY; JAMES HAMRICK; WILLIAM GARDNER; WM. TEBBS Sheriff for levies; JOHN HOLLIS; RICHD. ROLLINGS per judgment; CORNELIUS KINCHELOE; WILL. SEWELL per judgment; FRANS. SUMMERS, Consta. ..

. . . .. WILLIAM KING; JOHN WINDSOR; JNO. MINOR for Dr. HUNTER's Esta.; DANIEL LAUGHLIN his share; SAMPSON & HAGAR delivered ENOCH HILL his proportion; eight negroes (named) my proportion; paid BEN KENT for taking up a horse; 5 prs. Mourning gloves; ROBT. CARTER Esqr. for rent; (1765) WM. HALLEY'S share; JNO. OBRIAN'S share; Mr. THOMAS LAWSON; THOS. SUMMERS Constable; JNO. HOUGH for quit rents; JAMES LANE for tax & quit rents; MOSES CONGROVE; JNO. WINDSOR.

CONTRA. JNO. HARTSHORN; Col. JNO. WEST; THOMAS GRAFFORT; MOSES CONGROVE; BEN MASON; 1 pr Blk gloves. Balanced at £ 720.1.6.

At a court held .. 23rd March 1768 .. ELI CLEVELAND & MARY, his wife (Executrix of SAMUEL CANTERBURY, decd) exhibited this account and same being examined by the court is allowed and ordered to be Recorded.

pp. 19-22 1765. DR. The Estate of CHRISTOPHER NEALE, decd, to HENRY MOORE. Boarding HANNAH & THOMAS NEALE from Sepr. 1765; paid CHARLES TYLER Sheriff; Mr. WILLIAM CARR LANE; Waggoning Tobacco to Colchester; Mr. ALEXANDER HENDERSON; for THOMAS NEALE'S schooling; JOHN HOUGH for quit rents; Doctor NISBETT for Miss HANNAH; to Mr. HECTOR ROSS for Miss HANNAH; (also) THOMAS NEALE; Mrs. ANN GORHAM for making breeches; paid CRAVEN PEYTON; ROBERT ADAM; sundries delivered to Mr. HENDERSON guardian to the two children.

CONTRA. (1765. Paid the Sheriff of Loudoun; Mr. W.C. LANE; CRAVEN PEYTON'S Account. Account examined by WILLIAM RAMSAY, JOHN DALTON .. 23rd September 1767.

At a court held .. 25th March 1768 .. HENRY MOORE who intermarried with ANN NEALE, administratrix of CHRISTOPHER NEALE, decd, exhibited these accounts & same being examined by the court are allowed and ordered to be recorded.

pp. 22-23 1765. DR. CATHARINE, WILLIAM & JOHN GRIMES, orphans of WILLIAM GRIMES, decd. Goods bot of FLEMING PATTERSON; bot of HENRY RIDDLE .. no board allowed this year; omitted to charge in my last acct the schooling of (orphans).

At a court held .. 25th March 1768 .. GREENBERRY DORSEY who intermarried with CATHARINE GRIMES, administratrix of WILLIAM GRIMES, decd, exhibited this account .. same ordered to be recorded.

pp. 23-24 Will of ANN SIMONS. I ANN SIMONS of county of Fairfax and Town of Alexandria .. give and bequeath unto my well beloved friend, ROBERT JONES, of same county, Town and Colony all that sum of money together with the Interest thereon which I now have or is my right in the hands of Mr. ROBERT COLEMAN upon Little Tower Hill near St. Catharine's in the City of London in the Kingdom of Great Britain which sum was devised to me by Capn. STEPHEN BLACK WOOD of the Kingdom of great Britain .. also my other Estate of any kind .. I bequeath unto ROBERT JONES .. I appoint ROBERT JONES the only Executor of this my last will and testament .. this 6th day February 1768.

Presence: Francis Dade, Ann Simons
Edward Jones junr., Peter Perry,
William x Burnett

At a court held .. 25th March 1768 .. will presented by ROBERT JONES .. same being proved .. is ordered to be recorded.

pp. 24-25 We the Subscribers .. have appraised all the Estate of BENJAMIN GRAYSON, decd, which was presented to our view .. each item valued and totalled, £ 52.12.9. Given 30th March 1768 by HEN. MOORE, H. ROSS, A. HENDERSON.

. . . . Subscribers appraised estate of BENJAMIN GRAYSON, decd, in county of Loudoun .. each item valued and totalled, £ 155.15.0 .. given 16th April 1768 by appraisers WM. RUST, THO. OWSLEY, DAN. JONES.

At a court held .. 19th April 1768 .. inventories returned and ordered to be recorded.

pp. 26-27 Inventory & appraisement of the Estate of FRENCH MASON, deceased .. each item valued and totalled .. 1960 pounds Tobacco; £ 139.4.7½. Given 8th April 1768 by appraisers WILLIAM x MOORE, WILLIAM x LEATCH,

BENNETT HILL.
At a court held .. 16th May 1768 .. inventory returned and ordered to be recorded.

pp. 27-28 Will of THOMAS WREN. I THOMAS WREN of county of Fairfax .. give and bequeath unto my beloved son, NICHOLAS WREN, nineteen shillings current money; to my loving son, WILLIAM WREN, the Lease of land whereon I now live, two negroes after his Mother's death; unto my loving son, JOHN WREN, one negro boy after his Mother's death; to my loving son, TRAVERSE WREN, one negro boy after his Mother's death; to my loving son, ISAAC WREN, one negro girl and her future increase after his Mother's death; unto my loving daughter, WINNEY ATHILL, ten shillings current money she having had her full part before; to my loving daughter, ANN WREN, one negro garl & her future increase at her coming of age or day of marriage; unto my loving daughter, MARY WREN, one negro boy & one bed & furniture at her coming of age or day of marriage; I lend my dear & loving wife, JEAN WREN, the Lease of land whereon I live & seven negroes .. appoint my loving wife, JEAN WREN, Executrix, also my four sons, WILLIAM WREN, JOHN WREN, TRAVERSE WREN and ISAAC WREN, Executors with her .. this 8th day September 1767.
Presence: James Donaldson, Robert Lindsay, James Wren — Thos. Wren
At a court held .. 16th May 1768 .. will presented by JEAN WREN, WILLIAM WREN & JOHN WREN .. same being proved by witnesses is admitted to record .. certificate is granted them for obtaining a probate thereof ..

p. 29 Will of JOHN SHERIDON. I JOHN SHERIDON of Fairfax County .. give and bequeath to my loving wife, BARBARRY SHERIDON all my Estate .. except my waring cloaths, saddel & bridle which I give and bequeath unto my loving Father, JOHN SHERIDON .. this 6th day September 1767.
Witnesses: Samuel Johnston, Samuel Fielder — John Sheridin
At a court held .. 16th May 1768 .. will presented by BARBARA SHERIDON .. proved by oaths of witnesses .. admitted to record .. said BARBARA is granted certificate for obtaining a probate thereof ..

pp. 29-30 1768. Appraisement of JOHN HOLLIS estate, deceased .. each item valued and totalled, £ 22.17.7½. Signed and appraised by us the Subscribers ELI STONE, JOHN DULING, PHILIP GRIMES.
At a court held .. 17th May 1768 .. inventory returned and ordered to be recorded.

pp. 30-31 Appraisal of the things shown us (Estate of ALEXANDER MILLS) .. each item valued and totalled, £ 70.4.3 .. made 14th May 1768 by appraisers WM. GARDNER, WM. SIMPSON, JNO. ROBERTSON.
At a court held .. 17th May 1768 .. inventory returned and ordered to be recorded.

pp. 31-33 1766. Estate of Mr. JOSIAS MANKIN. DR. Paid JOHN PRESCOAT; paid RICHARD TUBMAN MANKIN; WILLIAM WOOLTON; ROBERT ADAM Sheriff; (1767) expenses from Maryland Vizt. ferriage to & from Maryland; ordinary expenses for myself & horse 3 days; paid Colo. GEORGE MASON his rent; paid SAMPSON DARRELL Sheriff parish levy due to WILLIAM PAYNE late Sheriff & cost of distress; paid Constable for crying the goods at sale.
CONTRA. By HENRY RIDDLE for 1 Tea Table bought at sale; SAMUEL JOHNSTON; JOHN McLAUGHLIN, JOHN RUFF, WILLIAM WOOLTON, JOHN McCROCKLIN;

SAMUEL JOHNSTON SENR.; JAMES BOYD; MARY MANKINS for sundries; ABEDNEGO ADAMS .. 13th May 1768.

At a court held .. 18th May 1768 .. ABEDNEGO ADAMS, administrator of JOSIAS MANKIN, decd, exhibited this account .. ordered to be recorded.

pp. 1763. Estate of RICHARD SIMPSON, decd. To Mr. EDWARD PAYNE for
33- Levys & Taxes; THOMAS WINDSOR; THOMAS WINDSOR JUNR.; JAMES HALLEY;
34 ELIZA. REED for attendance at funeral; Mr. GEORGE JOHNSTON; THOMAS POOR for Taylors work; SARAH SIMPSONS part of the estate deld her; To GEORGE SIMPSON; JAMES HALLEY; SAMUEL CANTERBURY; THOMAS WINDSOR; MOSES SIMPSON; RICHARD SIMPSON each £ 35.3.0; 11 negroes delivered all devisees; (1763) JOHN GRAHAMS rent; (1765) MOSES SIMPSON; GEO. SIMPSON; JOHN GRIMES; DAVID MILLER, JOSEPH YEATMAN; JOHN ALDERSON; CHS. CORNISH; WILLIAM BARKER; WILLIAM WILLIAMSON; WM. CONNELLY. Account totalled Tobacco 888 and £ 872.11.9.

At a court held .. 20th June 1768 .. GEORGE SIMPSON, one of the Executors of RICHARD SIMPSON, decd, exhibited this account .. is allowed and ordered to be recorded.

pp. 1767. The Estate of RICHARD OSBORN, Deced. Ballance of a settle-
34- ment made with the court the 19th June 1751; ballance of do 22nd May
35 1752; balance of do 21st August 1752; ballance of do 26th February 1755 .. £ 856.17.10¼; 26986 pounds Tobacco. Settlement made with Court 1766; paid WILLIAM ELLZEY fee ads BRIDGET CASTELLOE. To JOHN KING, Exr.

CR. Sale of whole amount of Estate as recorded 2d April 1751; £ 842.17.0; by TERRITT LITTLEJOHN, THOMAS LEWIS'S Estate ..

At a court held .. 19th July 1768 .. JOHN KING, Executor of the last will and testament of RICHARD OSBORN, decd, exhibited this account .. is allowed and ordered to be recorded.

p. Will of JOHN PATTERSON. I JOHN PATTERSON of ye Town of Alexandria,
35 Joiner, being in perfect health .. give to SUSANNA my Dearly beloved wife full power to possess every thing I am Possed of .. espescially two Lotts of land in Town of Alexandria numbered Fifty one & Fifty two .. while she remains a widow & to provide a suitable gente Education & Living for my three beloved children, WILLIAM, THOMAS & BETTY .. but in case ye sd SUSANNA my wife alters her state by matrimony (or any other Method not to ye advantage of my afsd children) to have no other part of my Estate but what the law allows (her thirds) .. I constitute SUSANNA, my wife, sole Executrix and after her death my two afsd lots of land to be sold and divided with ye other part of my Estate between my three children .. give my wife full power to purchase (in case I do not purchase before I go to Europe) a negro girl for my daughter, Betty .. this 6th day October 1765.

Presence: James Connell, Jno. Patterson
Richard Lake, Going Lamphier

At a court held .. August 15th 1768 .. will presented by SUSANNA PATTERSON .. proved by witnesses and is admitted to record .. certificate is granted her for obtaining a probate thereof in due form.

pp. We have valued & appraised all the Estate of THOMAS WREN, deceased,
37- that hath been presented to our view (this 28th of July 1768) .. each
38 item valued (including one pair of Spectecles) and totalled, £ 376.0.0 .. made by appraisers WM. PAYNE JR., JAMES DONALDSON, ROBT. LINDSAY.

At a court held .. 15th August 1768 .. inventory returned & ordered to be recorded.

pp. 38-39 An inventory of the Estate of JAMES KING, Deceased. Each item valued and totalled, £ 26.2.7, made by appraisers WILLIAM TALBUT, JOHN STONE, ROBERT THOMAS.
At a court held .. 17th August 1768 .. inventory returned and ordered to be recorded.

p. 39 Sales of the Estate of JAMES KING, August 19, 1766. Sold to JONATHAN DAINTY, THOMAS KIRBY, JOHN KING; a chest by GIDEON SMITH, 3 tubs by JOHN STONE, 1 bed by HENRY TALBOT, a heifer by W. SEWEL; LEONARD THOMAS, PETER SARTOR; DAVID HUGHES; GRAFTON KIRK; ROBT. HUMPHREYS; JOHN DALTON; ROBERT JONES; JOHN REYLEY; JOHN CARLYLE .. amount of sales £ 33.12.0½; Per JOHN CARLYLE,JOHN DALTON, JOHN KING.
At a court held .. 17th August 1768 .. sale returned and ordered to be recorded.

p. 40 We did meet & appraise all the Estate of JOHN SHERIDINE, Decd, that was brought to our view. Each item valued and totalled, £ 241. 7.3 .. made by appraisers SAMPSON DARRELL, THOMAS TRIPLETT, SAML. JOHNSTON.
At a court held .. 17th August 1768 .. inventory returned and ordered to be recorded.

p. 41 Will of JANE SHAW. I JANE SHAW of Fairfax County .. give to JOHN DALTON my negro man Jack; to JENNY DALTON and CATHERINE DALTON the rest of my estate due by bond and otherwise to be equally divided between them .. appoint my loving friend, JOHN DALTON, Executor .. this 12th day January 1768.
Jane x Shaw
Presence: E. Hunter, Thoms. Shaw
At a court held .. 17th August 1768 .. will presented by JOHN DALTON .. being proved is admitted to record .. certificate granted him for obtaining a probate thereof in due form.

pp. 41-42 We have appraised all the Goods and Chattles of WILLIAM DONALDSON, Decd, as were produced to our view .. each item valued and totalled, £ 67.10.10 .. made by appraisers W. PAYNE JR., EPHRAIM DICKEN & JOSEPH POWELL.
At a court held .. xixth Sepr. 1768 .. inventory returned and ordered to be recorded.

pp. 42-43 Estate of JOHN HOLLIS, Decd. DR. To PHILLIP GRIMES for appraising; paid ELY STONE; JOHN DULING; JOHN BARRAT. Totals 582 pounds Tobacco or £ 10.13.6½.
At a court held .. xxith Novr. 1768 .. EASTER HOLLIS, administratrix of Estate of JOHN HOLLIS, deceased, exhibited this account .. is allowed and ordered to be recorded.

p. 43 Sale of Estate of JOHN HOLLIS, deceased .. shows items sold and amount received .. amount of sale not totalled ..
At a court held .. xxith Novemr. 1768 .. Sale of Estate of JOHN HOLLIS, deceased, returned and ordered to be recorded.

pp. 44-45 Will of ROBERT THOMAS. The 12th day of January 1768 I ROBERT THOMAS of Fairfax County .. give and bequeath to my son, MOSES THOMAS, one feather bed & furniture and two cows & calves; to my well beloved wife, MARGARET THOMAS, one mare, side saddle & bridle, one sow and pigs and the Lease of the Plantation whereon I now live .. all the rest of my estate I desire to be sold .. and money bestowed as followeth. I leave to my son, ROBERT THOMAS, one shilling sterling;

to my son, AARON THOMAS, one shilling sterling; to my daughter, MARY MITCHEL, one shilling sterling; to my daughter, JEMIMA VOILET, one shilling sterling .. remainder of money to be equally divided between my well beloved wife and grandson, WILLIAM MITCHEL, my grandson, ROBERT THOMAS, & my granddaughter, ELIZABETH THOMAS, daughter of my son AARON THOMAS .. appoint my wife, MARGARET THOMAS, my son, AARON THOMAS, and JOHN RATCLIFF Executors ..

Presence: Ephraim Dicken, Robt. x Thomas

James Moxley, Thos. x Hawl, Wm. x Crump

At a court held .. 22d November 1768 .. will presented by AARON THOMAS .. being proved is ordered to be recorded .. certificate is granted him for obtaining a probate thereof in due form.

pp. 45-46 An inventory of the Estate of TIMOTHY LINES, Novr. 19th 1768. Items valued and totalled, ₤ 2.8.6 .. made by appraisers PRESLEY COX, RICHD. SANFORD, ROBT. SANFORD.

At a court held .. 23rd November 1768 .. inventory returned and ordered to be recorded.

pp. 46-47 We have valued and appraised all the Estate of ROBT. THOMAS, Deceased, as was presented to our view .. each item valued and totalled, ₤ 111.3.3 .. made by appraisers WM. PAYNE JR., JOSEPH POWELL, EPHRAIM DICKEN.

At a court held .. xxth February 1769 .. inventory returned and ordered to be recorded.

pp. 47-48 Will of JAMES ROBERTSON SENIOR. I JAMES ROBERTSON SENIOR of Fairfax County .. being old .. give and bequeath to my well beloved son, JOHN ROBERTSON, the tract of land I now live on containing 630 acres except in case that the Alexanders should obtain that tract of land adjoining Tods & Evans and if so be then my daughter JENNET BOWMAKER ROBERTSON is to have 320 acres of JOHN ROBERTSON'S land .. bequeath to my well beloved daughter, JENNET BOWMAKER ROBERTSON, the tract of land adjoining Todd & Evans containing 360 acres. To my granddaughter, ELIZABETH ROBERTSON, daughter to JAMES ROBERTSON JUNR., 100 acres of land beginning on four mile run .. remainder of said tract I give to my well beloved son, JAMES ROBERTSON.

N.B. I give to my son, JOHN ROBERTSON, my desk & to my daughter, JANNETT ROBERTSON, my round Table, and the rest of my goods .. equally divided between my wife, ELIZABETH ROBERTSON, and my daughter, JANNET BOWMAKER ROBERTSON and my son, JOHN ROBERTSON .. this 4th day of September 1768.

Presence Charles Craig, James Robertson Senr.

Nelson Reed, James x Mattenly

At a court held .. xxith Feby. 1769 .. will presented and proved and admitted to record .. ELIZABETH ROBERTSON, widow and relict of JAMES ROBERTSON, deceased, came into court and renounced all benefit by said will and on her motion and giving security Certificate is granted her for obtaining Letters of Administration with the will annexed ..

pp. 48-50 Will of WILLIAM FRIZEL. I WILLIAM FRIZEL of Fairfax Parish in county of Fairfax .. give and bequeath unto my loving son, JEASON FRIZEL, the sum of Ten pounds of lawfull money of Virginia; likewise to my daughter, SARY JONSON, the sum of Five shillings; likewise to my daughter, COMFORD YONG, the sum of Five shillings; to my loving friend and couzen, NATHAN FREZEL, all my hole estate that will remain after paying all my Legacies, I say all my personal estate such as Cattle, hogs, horses and all my household furniture and lastly appoint my said trusty and loving friend, NATHAN FRIZEL, to be my Executor ..

this 29th day July 1767.
Presence: Daniel Jenings, William x Frissell
Chas. Craig, John x Payne
At a court held .. 15th May 1769 .. will presented .. admitted to record .. certificate is granted Executor for obtaining a probate ..

pp. 50-52 Will of JANE TURLEY. I JANE TURLEY of Truro Parish in county of Fairfax .. give and bequeath to MARTHA TURLEY, the wife of my son, SAMPSON TURLEY, during her natural life the use of a negro girl .. after said MARTHA'S decease, negro girl and her Increase shall be equally divided amongst my grandchildren, HENRIETTA TURLEY, GILES TURLEY, MARTHA TURLEY, ANN TURLEY, SAMPSON TURLEY, JAMES TURLEY, ELIZABETH TURLEY and SUSANAH TURLEY .. but insomuch as said negro girl is only mortgaged to me by my son, SAMPSON TURLEY, for the sum of Forty pounds by Deed duly admitted to record in Fairfax Court which mortgage is not yet forfeited, If therefore my son, SAMPSON TURLEY, shall hereafter redeem the said girl by paying the Forty pounds within the time limited .. it is my will the Forty pounds shall be equally divided amongst all my said grandchildren .. I give MARTHA TURLEY, the wife of my son, SAMPSON TURLEY, my blew cloth cloak .. to my granddaughter, JEAN TURLEY, two feather beds and furniture as they shall be found standing below stairs at the time of my decease .. (also a number of other items) .. my suit of silk cloaths consisting of a Gown and Petticoat, my spinning wheel, Box iron and heaters and all the Wool & Cotton which shall be in the house spun and unspun .. to my granddaughter, HENRIETTA TURLEY, one feather bed and furniture as it shall be found standing in the second room above stairs .. (also other items) .. to my granddaughter, MARTHA TURLEY, one feather bed and furniture as the same shall be found standing in the first room above stairs .. to my granddaughter, ANN TURLEY, my other feather bed and furniture as the same shall be found standing in the closet .. to MARY WALDEN, my black Cumbarzine Gown and Petticoat .. to JOHN WALDEN, son of JOHN WALDEN and MARY, his wife, one three year old black Mare colt .. to my friend, JOHN TILLETT, one cow and calf.. to ELIZABETH CONNELL Twenty shillings current money .. to my grandson, JOHN TURLEY, my large Bible, to my grandson, GILES TURLEY, one three year old bay mare .. it is my will all my wearing apparel (except what is already given and such as I may hereafter think fit to bequeath by word of mouth) shall be equally divided between my two granddaughters, JANE TURLEY and HENRIETTA TURLEY .. residue of my Estate to be sold .. money I give to my grandson, JOHN TURLEY, to be paid him by my Executors at his age of twenty one and not before .. it being my desire the money shall remain till that time in the hands of my Executors. I appoint my much esteemed friend, Mr. ALEXANDER HENDERSON, Merchant, and JOHN TILLETT, Executors .. this 8 day September 1768.
Presence: Elijah Williams, Jane x Turley
John Simpson, Moses Simpson
At a court held .. 15th May 1769 .. will presented (by Executors) .. admitted to record and on motion of Executors .. certificate is granted them for obtaining a probate thereof in due form.

pp. 52-53 Inventory of the Estate of WILLIAM FRIZDELL, decd, May 20th 1769 .. items valued and totalled, £ 27.16.1½ .. made by appraisers CHARLES CRAIG, GEORGE THRIFT, JOSEPH x EARP.
At a court held .. 19th June 1769 .. inventory returned and ordered to be recorded.

pp. 53-55 Will of SAMUEL JOHNSTON. I SAMUEL JOHNSTON of Fairfax County .. give and bequeath unto my loving son, SAMUEL JOHNSTON, one negro woman .. one negro girl .. after his death I give the negro girl unto my granddaughter, HANNAH, daughter of my son, SAMUEL JOHNSTON .. I give my son, SAMUEL JOHNSTON, one half of my weareing apparell .. one negro man at the death of my wife or at the end of her widowhood. I give and bequeath unto my loving son, JOHN JOHNSTON, one negro girl, one feather bed and furniture & the other half of my wareing apparel .. also a negro boy after the death of my wife .. unto my loving daughter, SUSANAH JOHNSTON, one negro girl, one feather bed and furniture and Thirty pounds Virginia currency to be paid unto her when she demands it .. also a negro man after death of my wife .. I give unto my daughter, HANNAH JOHNSTON, one negro girl, one feather bed and furniture and Thirty pounds Virginia currency to be paid her whenever she demands it .. also a negro man after death of my wife .. I give unto my loving daughter, FRANCIS CLEAVELAND, a negro boy and after the death of my daughter unto my grandson, JOHNSTON CLEAVELAND .. also a negro girl after the death of my wife .. and half a dozen sheep to be delivered in April 1770 .. unto my son in law, JAMES CLEAVELAND, eleven or twelve pounds current money which he borrowed from me .. unto my loving daughter, TAMER SIMPSON, a negro boy .. after her death to my grandson, SAMUEL SIMPSON. I give unto my loving daughter, ANN THOMPSON, one negro girl .. also unto my son in law, JOSEPH THOMPSON, his note of hand payable unto me for fifteen Pistoles .. negro girl to descend to my grandson, SAMUEL THOMPSON. I give unto my sons, SAMUEL JOHNSTON and JOHN JOHNSTON, all my Coopers tools to be equally divided .. I give unto my loving wife, HANNAH JOHNSTON, all the residue of my estate .. also appoint my loving wife, HANNAH JOHNSTON, and my son, SAMUEL JOHNSTON, Executrix and Executor .. this first day May 1769.

Presence: John Orr,
Joseph Thompson, Thomas Triplett

Samuel x Johnston

At a court held .. 19th June 1769 .. will presented by (Executors) .. admitted to record .. certificate is granted them for obtaining a probate thereof in due form.

pp. 55-57 Will of JOHN McINTOSH. The 23d day of May 1769, I JOHN McINTOSH of Fairfax County and Town of Colchester .. give and bequeath to my son, LOCHLIN McINTOSH .. my lots and Houses in the Town of Colchester. I give to my son, JOHN McINTOSH .. my old plantation where WILLIAM McDONALL now lives containing 93 acres. I give to my son, THOMAS McINTOSH, my new tract of land with 100 acres thereto belonging where old JAMES McDANIEL now lives .. if my three sons die before age twenty one my desire is that my land be equally divided among my three daughters .. (bequests of land to his sons each carry provision .. after my youngest daughter shall arrive to age of eighteen years) .. my desire the remaining part of my Estate shall be equally divided between my three daughters, CATHARINE, ANN & VALINDER McINTOSH, when the youngest shall come to age but my wife shall have the management of the whole during that time in order to support the young children .. appoint my wife, ELIZABETH McINTOSH, and LOCHLIN McINTOSH, my Executors ..

Presence: Alex. Henderson, H. Ross,
Ed. Washington, Samuel Stone, Pet. Wagener

John McIntosh

At a court held .. 20th June 1769 .. will presented by ELIZABETH McINTOSH .. proved by Hector Ross and Alexander Henderson and is ordered to be recorded .. certificate is granted her for obtaining letters of administration with will annexed ..

pp. 57-59 We have inventoried and appraised such of Estate of JOHN McINTOSH, Decd, as was brought to our view by ELIZABETH McINTOSH, Executrix, this 5th day of July 1769 .. items valued and totalled, £ 144.3.6 .. made by appraisers WILLIAM BAYLY, HEN: MOORE, WILLIAM x REARDON.

At a court held .. 18th July 1769 .. inventory returned and ordered to be recorded.

pp. 59-61 We the Subscribers being first sworn did meet and appraise all the Estate of SAMUEL JOHNSTON, Deceased, that was brought to our vue. Items valued and totalled, £ 989.3.6 .. made by appraisers SAMPSON DARRELL, HUMPHREY PEAKE, WM. TRIPLETT.

At a court held .. 21st August 1769 .. inventory returned and ordered to be recorded.

pp. 61-62 1768. DR. The Estate of SAMUEL CANTERBURY, deceased .. paid Mr. ALEXANDER HENDERSON as per judgment; paid GEORGE SIMPSON as per acct. CONTRA. .. balance due estate on Settlement 23rd Marc 1768, £ 81.15.1, E. Exd. per ELY CLEAVELAND.

At a court held .. 21st August 1769 .. ELI CLEVELAND exhibited this account .. was allowed and ordered to be recorded.

pp. 62-63 The following is an Inventory of THOMS. SCOTTS Tools in the possession of Mr. CARLIN .. items valued and totalled, £ 11.1.10½ .. made by appraisers GOING LAMPHIER, WM. MUNDAY, THOS. BROWNLY.

At a court held .. 23rd Augt. 1769 .. inventory returned and ordered to be recorded.

pp. 63-66 An Inventory of the Estate of ROBERT JONES, deceased, taken the 29th day of March 1769 .. items valued and totalled, £ 189.13.1 .. some items .. a blew cotton Velvet waistcoat; a cloath Waistcoat with a dozen plate Buttons; an old Black Velvet Ditto; an old Red waistcoat; a pair of scarlet knitt Britches; an old Cloath jacket; gold silver and paper money in the house at Robert Jones's death, £ 35.15.9; 50 gall. rum; 100 gall. Cyder; 3 gall. wine; a pr. of Billiard balls .. made by appraisers WM. RAMSAY, RICHARD ARELL, JOHN MUIR.

At a court held .. 19th September 1769 .. inventory returned and ordered to be recorded.

pp. 66-68 Will of WILLIAM MOORE. I WILLIAM MOORE of County of Fairfax .. desire that my Executrix if she shall think there is more stock belonging to my estate than she can maintain do dispose of all or any part and one half of the money I give to my son, JAMES MOORE .. the other half I give the use thereof during her natural life to my loving wife, MARY MOORE & after her death I give to my son, JAMES MOORE, but if my Executrix should not dispose of the whole or any part of my Stock I give to my said wife, MARY MOORE, the whole or that part which shall remain unsold to use during her life so long as she shall remain a widow .. after I give all said Stock to my son, JAMES MOORE. To my wife, four slaves .. after her death to my son, JAMES .. my will that the mortgages I have on the lands of JOHN ANDERSON be foreclosed according to law which said lands I give to my son, JAMES. I give unto my son, SAMUEL MOORE, one shilling sterling; unto my daughter, SARAH LITTLEJOHN, (same) .. unto my daughter, MARY BUCKLIN, (same) .. unto my daughter, AN TYLER, (same) .. residue of my estate to my loving wife, MARY MOORE, after her death I give to my son, JAMES MOORE. I appoint my loving wife, MARY MOORE, Executrix, and my loving son, JAMES MOORE,

Executor .. this 17th August 1769 ..
Presence: A. Nisbett, William x Moore
Cleon Moore, John x Haise
At a court held .. 16th October 1769 .. will presented by MARY MOORE and JAMES MOORE .. is admitted to record .. Certificate is granted them for obtaining a probate thereof in due form.

pp. 68-70 Will of VENUS LAMPHIER. I VENUS LAMPHIER of Prince George County Maryland .. give unto my neice, BETTY PATTERSON, 100 pounds Irish currency out of the sum of 400 pounds same currency due me in Ireland .. I give to my said Niece, BETTY, and my nephews, WILLIAM & THOMAS PATTERSON, one equal third share a piece of the remainder .. if my Executrix shall receive less than the 400 pounds Irish currency due me .. my neice, BETTY, shall have 100 pounds same currency & the residue equally divided .. if my Executrix shall receive more than the 100 pounds, my niece, BETTY, shall receive 100 pounds and the remainder equally divided .. if either of the said children, BETTY, WILLIAM & THOMAS PATTERSON, shall die without heirs, that my sister, SUSANAH PATTERSON, shall have the whole. I give unto my brother, GOING LAMPHIER, five shillings Irish currency. I appoint my sister, SUSANA PATTERSON, my sold Executrix .. this 14th day February 1769.
Declared by said VENUS LAMPHIER as her last will .. in presence of Venus Lamphier
James Kirk, John Rister, Mary x Rister, Richard x Neele
At a court held .. 24th November 1769 .. will presented by SUSANA PATTERSON, Executrix .. admitted to record .. Certificate is granted her for obtaining a probate thereof in due form.

pp. 70-71 Will of ROBERT SANFORD. I ROBERT SANFORD of county of Fairfax .. give unto my beloved wife, ELIZABETH SANFORD, all the use and benefit of my whole Estate during her widowhood after which I give to my beloved son, RICHARD SANFORD .. and one negro man .. also to my son, WILLIAM SANFORD, I give one negro man .. to my son, ROBERT SANFORD, I give one negro man .. to my son, JAMES, I give one negro man .. to my son, JOHN SANFORD, I give one negro boy .. to my son, EDWARD, I give one negro boy .. to my daughter, Francis Sanford, I give one negro girl & one negro boy .. the residue of my slaves I leave equally divided among my following children after my wife's death or widowhood, Vizt. ROBERT, JAMES, JOHN and EDWARD SANFORD .. all my land I bequeath to my son, RICHARD .. this 23d day March 1769. I appoint my sons, RICHARD, WILLIAM and ROBERT, Executors ..
Presence: John West junr., Robert Sanford
Presley Cox, Charles Jones,
Wm. Baker, Henry Darne
At a court held .. xxith November 1769 .. will presented by (Executors) .. admitted to record .. Certificate is granted them for obtaining a probate thereof in due form.

pp. 71-73 We the Subscribers being first sworn did appraise such of the Estate of ROBERT SANFORD, decd, as was produced to our view .. items valued and totalled, £ 664.1.7 .. given 12th December 1769 by JOHN DALTON, DANIEL TALBOTT, SAMPSON DARRELL. A supplementary inventory with items not valued given 18th December 1769 by RICHARD SANFORD, WILLIAM SANFORD, R. SANFORD JUNR.
At a court held .. 18th December 1769 .. inventory returned and ordered to be recorded.

pp. 73-74 Will of MARY JOHNSTON. I MARY JOHNSTON, Widow .. give unto my granddaughter, MARY MASSEY, all my whole Estate .. and appoint LEE MASSEY, Executor .. this 20th November 1769.
Presence: He. Lane, Mary x Johnston
The mark JL of Jane Leach
At a court held .. 18th December 1769 .. will presented by LEE MASSEY .. further proved by Hardage Lane who made oath that he read the same to MARY JOHNSTON who said she heard it & that it was right that he saw her sign the said Will and heard her declare the same to be her last will and testament & that he, the said Hardage Lane, at the request of the Testatrix and in her presents did subscribe the same .. that said Testatrix was of sound and Disposing mind and memory .. further made oath he saw JANE LEACH (who is since dead) subscribe the same .. Certificate is granted him for obtaining a probate thereof in due form.

pp. 74-75 Estate of FRENCH MASON, Deceased. DR. Paid Mr. JOHN MERCER by Penal Bill; paid GEORGE MASON, Gent.; ALEXANDER HENDERSON; HECTOR ROSS; JAMES SIMONDS; ROBERT BRENT; JAMES NISBETT; JOHN HOUGH; DANIEL McCARTY; VALENTINE CLONINGER; THOMAS MARSHALL; JAMES BROWN.
CONTRA. Amount of inventory Tobo. 1968; £ 139.4.7½; by CUMBERLAND WILSON, £ 13.4.9. ANN MASON, Administratrix.
At a court held .. 19th December 1769 .. ANN MASON, Administratrix of FRENCH MASON, deceased, exhibited this account .. is allowed and ordered to be recorded.

p. 75 We the Subscribers being first sworn on the Holy Evangelist have made out an inventory of the Goods of BRIDGETT CASTELLO that were brought to our view and have appraised the same & is hereunto annexed .. March 16, 1769 .. items valued and totalled, £ 15.8.4½ .. made by appraisers MICHL. GRETTER, THOS. BROWNLY, JAMES CONNELL.
At a court held .. 21st February 1770 .. inventory returned and ordered to be recorded.

p. 76 DR. BRIDGET CASTELLO decd in Acct with WILLIAM RAMSAY. To account given in by WM. TRIPLETT 28th day of Feby 1776; one years house rent March 1st 1767; coffin; digging grave; my trouble, £ 1.10.10½.
CONTRA. By JAS. STRICKLAND, GEORGE McKNESS; attending PETERS wife; Mrs. RAMSAY, GEO. JOHNSTON; your son; Mrs. KEY .. account balances, £ 32.8.8 3/4.
At a court held .. 21st February 1769 .. WILLIAM RAMSAY, Gent., administrator of BRIDGET CASTELLO, deced, exhibited this account .. is allowed & ordered to be recorded.

pp. 76-78 We the Subscribers being appointed and first sworn have met valued and appraised the Estate of Mr. EDWARD DAVIS, Deceased, and find the Particulars and value as follows .. items valued but not totalled .. made by appraisers GERRARD TRAMMELL, ROBERT LINDSAY, JOSEPH MOXLEY.
At a court held .. 16th April 1770 .. inventory returned and ordered to be recorded.

pp. 78-79 Will of JOSHUA FERGUSON. I JOSHUA FERGUSON of County of Fairfax and parish of Truro .. desire that my just debts be paid and the residue of my Estate be equally divided amongst all my children, Vizt. JOHN FERGUSON, ANN FERGUSON, JUDEY FERGUSON, JOSHUA FERGUSON, MARY FERGUSON, JOSEPH FERGUSON, ELIZABETH FERGUSON, WILLIAM FERGUSON and the child that my loving wife, MARY FERGUSON, is big with .. that my son, JOHN FERGUSON, do receive one half of his proportionable part as soon as a division can be made .. the other half remain in the hands of my loving wife, MARY FERGUSON, so long as she shall remain a widow & no longer .. my will & desire that my loving Friends, WILLIAM STONE, JAMES MOORE & MARCELLUS LITTLEJOHN, do alot & equally divide my whole estate among my children & I do appoint my loving wife, MARY FERGUSON, and my loving son, JOHN FERGUSON, my hole & sole Executors .. this first day of January 1770.

Presence: Chas. Broadwater, Joshua Ferguson
William Stone, Gabriel x Baxter

At a court held .. 16th April 1770 .. will presented by MARY FERGUSON .. is admitted to record .. a Certificate is granted her for obtaining a probate thereof in due form.

pp. 79-80 We the Subscribers being appointed to appraise the Estate of VENUS LAMPHIER, deceased .. do make the following appraisement .. items valued and totalled, £ 32.12.0 .. includes 6 Callico & Cotton Gowns & Sacks, 2 white Callico Do (1 old), 1 black Crape Do, 1 large Velvet Capuchin, one new hat and an old silk bonnett, 1 pr. stays & 1 pr. Jumps, 1 Callamanco petticoat, 1 pr. Silver buckles, 2 plain gold rings, 1 stone Gold ring (broke), 1 pr. Callamanco shoes .. made by appraisers JOHN DALTON, HARRY PIPER, JAMES CONNELL.

At a court held .. 24th May 1770 .. inventory returned & ordered to be recorded.

pp. 80-81 We the Subscribers being appointed to appraise the Estate of JOHN PATTERSON, deceased .. do make the following appraisement .. items valued and totalled, £ 236.3.3 .. includes JAMES JACKSON a servant who had about 15 months to serve .. made by appraisers HARRY PIPER, JOHN MUIR, JAMES CONNELL.

At a court held .. 24th May 1770 .. inventory returned and ordered to be recorded.

pp. 81-84 We the Subscribers being first duly sworn before CHARLES BROADWATER, Gent., have valued & appraised all the Estate of JOSHUA FERGUSON, Decd, that was brought to our view .. items valued and totalled, £ 535.3.8 .. made by appraisers WILLIAM STONE, JAMES MOORE, MARCELLUS LITTLEJOHN.

At a court held .. 18th June 1770 .. inventory returned and ordered to be recorded.

pp. 84-85 We the Subscribers have appraised Goods and Chattles of JOHN WATSON, deced .. items valued and totalled, £ 25.6.6 .. made by appraisers JOHN SUMMERS, JOHN RATCLIFF, WILLIAM SUMMERS.

At a court held .. 20th August 1770 .. inventory returned & ordered to be recorded.

pp. 85-86 June 20th 1770. The Estate of JOSHUA FERGUSON, Decd. DR .. paid ALEXANDER HENDERSON; LUTENER MIDDLETON; DRAKEFORD GRAY; HECTOR ROSS, Gent., WILLIAM GEORGE; JAMES NISBETT, TEMPLE SMITH, BENJA. HITCHINSON WEST; BENONI HALLEY; JOHN GOLLATT SMITH; Collo. GEORGE MASON Gent. for rent; the parish collector; GABRIEL BAXTER (overseer his share); paper and ink powder; Mr. WILLIAM BALMAIN.

CONTRA. Cash rec'd of GABRIEL BAXTER; WILLIAM SCOTT; JOHN WALLER; BENONI HAWLEY; JOSEPH BENNETT ..

At a court held .. 21st August 1770 .. MARY FERGUSON, Executrix of JOSHUA FERGUSON, Decd, exhibited this account .. is allowed and ordered to be recorded.

pp. We the Subscribers being first sworn did proceed to appraise the
86- Estate of DAVID YOUNG .. items valued and totalled, £ 77.3.2½ .. made
88 by appraisers JOHN DALTON, JOHN WEST JUNR., THOMAS FLEMING, CHARLES
JONES .. includes a silver watch ..

At a court held .. 22nd August 1770 .. inventory returned & ordered to be recorded.

pp. DR. The Estate of JAMES KING to CARLYLE & DALTON, Admrs. .. a
88- balance due from JAMES KING; CATHARINE WILDMAN hireling; WILLIAM GARD-
89 NER; LEONARD THOMAS; JOHN HUMPHREYS share; Mr. JOHN MUIR bond; Mr.
Robt. Adam.

CR. By THOMAS KERBY; JOHN REYLEY; H. RIDDELL for DAINTY; ROBT. JONES; ROBT. HUMPHREYS; JOHN DALTON; GRAFTON KIRK, LEONARD THOMAS & SARTER; DAVID HUGHES & JOHNSTON; JOHN CARLYLE, WILLIAM RAMSAY. Account balances £ 27.13.10. Balance due from Estate Tobo. 1393; £ 0.3.0.

At a court held .. 23rd August 1770 .. JOHN CARLYLE & JOHN KING, Administrators of JAMES KING, deceased, exhibited this account .. is allowed & ordered to be recorded.

pp. 1761 Feby. DR. The Estate of JOHN MINOR, Gent., to JOHN DALTON,
89- Executor .. to Mr. JOHN WEST Sheriff; cash paid ROBERT PETER; Mr. WIL-
90 LIAM PAYNE fee on Barnes Exec.; Mr. ROBT. ADAM; (1768) Mr. SAMPSON
DARRELL; (1769) Mr. WM. ADAMS; ABRAM BARNES & SARAH, his wife Decree in Chancery & Costs; Mr. JOHN WEST Surveying; commission for my trouble.

CONTRA. 1763 Aug 1. ABRAHAM BARNES for judgment against Estate of DENNIS McCARTY, Gent., with Interest and Costs; cash received from DOWNMANS Exers. Note that the Negroes amounting to £ 240.10 by appraisement was ordered by the Court to be delivered and divided among the widow & children ..

At a court held .. 23d August 1770 .. JOHN DALTON, Exer. of JOHN MINOR, Decd, exhibited this account .. is allowed and ordered to be recorded.

pp. Will of JAMES DONALDSON. I JAMES DONALDSON of parish of Truro and
90- county of Fairfax made this 8th day of September 1761 .. give and be-
91 queath to my son, STEPHEN DONALDSON, one negro boy .. unto MILDRED
DONALDSON, my granddaughter who is the only daughter of my son, WILLIAM DONALDSON, deceased, the sum of one shilling sterling .. residue of my estate to be equally divided among my children, STEPHEN DONALDSON, JOHN DONALDSON, DANIEL DONALDSON, BAILY DONALDSON and JANE DONALDSON .. appoint my loving wife, ANN DONALDSON, sole Executrix ..

Presence: Richard Rigg, William Shortridge, William Darne, John Shortridge

James Donaldson

At a court held .. 15th October 1770 .. will presented by ANN DONALDSON .. ordered to be recorded .. Certificate is granted her for obtaining a probate thereof in due form.

pp. Inventory of the Estate of Mr. WILLIAM MOORE, Decd, appraised by
92- WILLIAM LINTON, WILLIAM COURTS & WILLIAM REARDON being first duly
93 sworn before HECTOR ROSS, Gent. .. items valued and totalled, £ 484.1.
5½ ..

At a court held .. 19th November 1770 .. inventory returned and ordered to be recorded.

pp. 93-95 DR The Estate of Mr. WILLIAM MOORE to his Executors. To WILLIAM LINTON, JAMES MOORE, THOMAZIN ELLZEY, JOHN REILEY, Mr. HECTOR ROSS for DOCTOR NISBETT'S Acct., JOHN HAISE overseer for his share of crop, to COLO. GEORGE MASON for rent, three slaves bequeathed to the widow, Mrs. MARY MOORE for her life & the reversion to JAMES MOORE. Contra. sundry new goods from Mr. DEAKINS store in George Town Maryland applyed to the use of the widow, Mrs. MARY MOORE, Mr. HENRY MOORE, WILLIAM CULLINSON, ELIJAH WOOD, Mr. JAMES HALLEYS bond (when received) ..

At a court held .. xixth November 1770 .. JAMES MOORE and MARY MOORE, Exers. of WILLIAM MOORE, deceased, exhibited this account .. is allowed and ordered to be recorded.

pp. 95-96 Will of BENJAMIN SEBASTIAN SENIOR. I BENJAMIN SEBASTIAN SENIOR of county of Fairfax attorney at law do this 13th day of September 1770 ordain the following my last will and testament .. I give and devise unto my dear wife, PRISCILLA SEBASTIAN, all that parcel of land whereon I now live known by the name of Montpelier .. also slaves .. after my wife's death the land called Montpelier unto my two daughters, ELIZABETH and BEHETHELEM SEBASTIAN to be equally divided .. my land in county of Loudoun containing 350 acres be sold in fee simple by my friends, THOMAS LEWIS and JOHN MOSS, for payment of my just debts whom I appoint my Exers. for that purpose .. my tract of land in Fairfax County containing 150 acres which I purchased of BLANCH DUNCAN and LETTICE, his wife, shall be sold in fee simple for the payment of my just Debts by my friends, THOMAS WREN and WILLIAM WREN whom I appoint my Exers. for that purpose ..

Presence: Platt Townsend, Benja. Sebastian
Rob. H: Harrison, Mordock McPherson

At a court held .. xixth November 1770 .. will proved and ordered to be recorded.

pp. 96-99 We the Subscribers .. do appraise the Estate of JAMES DONALDSON, Deced .. items valued and totalled, £ 606.12.10½ .. made by appraisers HENRY GUNNELL, WM. SHORTRIDGE, GEORGE SHORTRIDGE ..

At a court held .. xxth November 1770 .. Inventory returned & ordered to be recorded.

p. 99 We the Subscribers do appraise three slaves they being the only effects or Estate presented to our view as the property of the late MARY JOHNSTON, widow, Deced .. each valued and totalled, £ 75 .. made by appraisers Rd. Harrison, Thomas Fleming, Chas. Turner.

At a court held .. 21st November 1770 .. inventory returned and ordered to be recorded.

pp. 99-101 We the Subscribers being first sworn before ALEXANDER HENDERSON, Gent. .. have Inventoryed and appraised all & singular the Estate of WILLIAM LINTON deced presented to our view .. items valued and totalled, £ 41.12.2 .. made by appraisers WM. COURTS, PET. WAGENER, PIERCE BAYLY .. among items .. an English Dixonary 7/6; an old Bible 3/; 4 bee hives ..

At court held .. 17th December 1770 .. inventory returned & ordered to be recorded.

pp. 101-102 Will of EWEL VILET. I EWEL VOILET of Fairfax County .. give and bequeath unto my loving wife, SIBYL VILET .. all the use benefit and advantage of my whole estate .. after her death or marriage my whole estate be sold at publick sale .. money equally divided amongst my children .. the boys to receive their part at age of Eighteen and the girls .. age Sixteen .. my desire my loving wife, SIBYL VILET & my son, WM. VIOLET, be Executors .. this 21st day November 1770.

Witnesses: William Cash, Wm. Triplett, Robt. x Williams, Eleanor x Culverhouse — Ewel x Vilet

At a court held .. 21st January 1771 .. will presented by SIBYL VIOLET .. admitted to record .. certificate is granted her for obtaining a probate thereof in due form.

pp. 102-103 Will of JAMES BOWMAKER. November 10th 1770. I JAMES BOWMAKER of Virginia Fairfax County .. give and bequeath to my well beloved cousin, JENNET BOWMAKER ROBERTSON, daughter of JAMES ROBERTSON SENR. seven pounds current money exclusive wife to JAMES ROBERTSON deced .. the rest of my estate to be equally divided between ELIZABETH ROBERTSON and JANNET BOWMAKER ROBERTSON and JOHN ROBERTSON, son to JAMES ROBERTSON SENIOR ..

Presence: John Ball, Mary x Cook, Charles Craig — James Bowmaker

MOSES BALL appointed to see JANNET BOWMAKER ROBERTSON receive her money. ELIZABETH ROBERTSON, Executrix.

At a court held .. 21st January 1771 .. will presented by ELIZABETH ROBERTSON .. admitted to record .. certificate is granted her for obtaining probate thereof in due form.

pp. 103-104 DR. The Estate of SAMUEL CANTERBURY, Decd .. paid EDWARD BENNETT for his judgment & costs; to Mr. ALEXANDER HENDERSON per Judgment..

At a court held .. 10th March 1771 .. ELI CLEVELAND, Exer. of SAMUEL CANTERBURY, Decd, exhibited this account .. is allowed & ordered to be recorded.

pp. 104-106 Will of THOMAS DOWDALL. I THOMAS DOWDALL of the County and Parish of Fairfax .. lend to my well beloved wife, MARTHA DOWDALL, all that I die possessed of .. after her decease to be divided between my children .. to my son, GEORGE DOWDALL, I leave the one half of my Loudoun tract of land that I bought of Mr. STURMAN whereon he now lives .. to my son, THOMAS DOWDALL, the other half of the aforesaid tract of land .. to be divided by a Hiccory corner to WM. MURRY .. if THOMAS DOWDALL should die .. said land to go to my grandson, THOMAS DOWDALL, son of George .. to my son, JOHN DOWDALL, the one half of the land I now live on, the other half I give to my son, JAMES DOWDALL, to be divided .. by a course of my lease .. JOHN DOWDALL to have the part I now live on, JAMES DOWDALL the other part .. to my sons, JAMES & JOHN DOWDALL, my copper still, tight casks, cart & Carpenters and Coopers Tools .. if they disagree on division my will is that they be sold to highest bidder at publick vendue & the money equally divided .. to my daughter, MARY GRIMES, five pounds .. to my daughter, CATHARINE HUBBARD, the money & goods which I lent her .. to my daughter, APHIA DOWDALL, Twenty pounds .. (and other items) to be paid on her day of marriage .. to my son, GEORGE DOWDALL, my wearing apparel .. remaining part of my Estate be sold to pay debts and legacies and anything remaining to be equally divided between my children .. appoint my two sons, JOHN & JAMES DOWDALL, Executors .. this 17th day December 1769.

Presence: Jas. Wren, Robt. Lindsay, Garrard x Trammell, Suckey x Frissell — Thomas Dowdall

In Codicil gives sum of Ten pounds current money of Virginia to daughter, ELIZABETH HUBBARD ..

p. An inventory of the Goods & Chattles of Mr. JAMES BOWMAKER, de-
107 ceased .. made by appraisers GEORGE THRIFT, NELSON REED, JAMES ROBERTSON .. a few items each valued and totaled, £ 5.2.4 ..
At a court held .. 20th March 1771 .. inventory returned and ordered to be recorded.

pp. Will of ANTHONY CROSSWAIT. This fourth day of March 1771, I
107- ANTHONY CROSSWHITE of Town of Alexandria, Marriner .. give and bequeath
108 unto my well beloved wife, ELIZABETH, all & singular the whole of my Estate .. and after her decease to be disposed of all she shall think most proper. I appoint my dearly beloved wife, ELIZABETH, my Executrix.
Presence of John Carlyle, John Orr   Anthy. x Crosswait
At a court held .. xxith May 1771 .. will presented by ELIZABETH CROSTHWAITE .. admitted to record .. certificate is granted her for obtaining a probate thereof ..

pp. Will of GEORGE DARRELL. March 30th 1771. GEORGE DARRELL'S will
108- and desire in presence of his Mother, MARY DARRELL and VALINDA WADE
109 is that his Brother, PHILIP DARRELL, should have all his estate after paying his just debts.
This day before me, MARY DARRELL & VALINDA WADE & made oath on the Holy Evangelist that the above writing was the last will of GEORGE DARRELL. Certified under my hand this 2d day April 1771.
Sampson Darrell
At a court held .. 20th May 1771 .. will presented by SAMPSON DARRELL .. is ordered to be recorded and on his motion certificate is granted him for obtaining letters of administration with the will annexed ..

pp. Will of JOHN DOGIN. I JOHN DOGIN of the county of Fairfax .. give
109- and bequeath to my two sons, HENRY DOGIN & JOHN DOGIN, three negroes
111 .. also eight head of cattle .. my will that negroes and stock be kept on my plantation whereon I now live until my son, HENRY DOGEN, shall attain the age of twenty one years during which time what profits may arise may be applyed to the educating & maintaining my two sons .. to my son, HENRY, my plantation whereon I now live he suffering his Brother, JOHN DOGINS, part of the negroes .. lend unto my wife, ELIZABETH DOGIN .. appoint my wife, ELIZABETH, & my son, HENRY, and Mr. ALEXANDER HENDERSON my Exers .. this first day of December 1770 ..
Presence of John Thornton,   John Dogon
James Lewis Gibbs, Mical x Holbert
Thos. Lucas, Anthony Rayns
At a court held .. 20th May 1771 .. will presented by ELIZABETH DOGAN .. is admitted to record .. certificate is granted her for obtaining a probate thereof ..

pp. We the Subscribers, MICHAEL GRETTER, JOHN CANNON & THOS. BROWNLY
111- being appointed .. to appraise the Estate of WILLIAM SEWELL decd have
112 appraised all that has been brought to our view .. items valued and totalled, £ 32.1.0 ..
At a court held .. 20th May 1771 .. inventory returned and ordered to be recorded.

pp. We the Subscribers being first sworn before Mr. ALEXANDER HENDER-
112- SON, Gent. have appraised the Estate of JAMES TURLEY Deceased that was
113 brought to our view in Current money .. items valued and totalled, £ 54.12.0 .. made by appraisers WILLIAM SIMPSON SENR., JOHN SIMPSON, JOHN TILLETT ..
At a court held .. 21st May 1771 .. inventory returned and ordered to be recorded.

pp. 113-114 A copy of the Appraisement of JOHN HOLLINGHEAD Decd Estate .. September 20th 1770 .. items valued and totalled, ₤ 8.0.6, made by appraisers EDWARD FORD, BAXTER SIMPSON, GEORGE TILLETT.

A copy of the sale of JOHN HOLLINGHEAD deceased Estate .. DR. Mr. Thomas Sangster, Mr. Edward Ford, Mr. William Gardner, Mr. Baxter Simpson, Mr. George Tillett, Mr. Moses Simpson, John Hamilton, John Kinner ..

At a court held .. 22d May 1771 .. inventory and appraisement returned and ordered to be recorded.

pp. 114-115 1770. Augt. 7. DR. JOHN HOLLONSHEAD Decd.

At a court held .. 22nd May 1771. MOSES SIMPSON, Administrator of JOHN HOLLENSHEAD Decd exhibited this account .. is allowed and ordered to be recorded.

p. 115 We the Subscribers have met valued and appraised the Estate of JOHN LOWE, Deceased, and find the particulars and value as follows .. items valued and totaled, ₤ 7.6.4¼ .. made by appraisers WILLIAM x HARDIN, JAMES x GREEN, DANIEL x JENNINGS ..

At a court held .. xixth August 1771. Inventory returned and ordered to be recorded.

pp. 115-117 Inventory of the goods & chattels which were of ANTHONY CROSWAITE late of Town of Alexandria in county of Fairfax deceased which was presented to the view of the Subscribers .. items valued and totalled, ₤ 85.7.10 .. appraisers JONA. HALL, JAMES CONNELL, CHAS. TURNER ..

At a court held .. xixth day August 1771 .. inventory returned and ordered to be recorded.

pp. 117-118 Will of RICHARD KENT. I RICHARD KENT of Fairfax County in good state of health .. I think it necessary to settle the affairs of this life .. give to my well beloved wife, ELLINER, during her widowhood acounting it so long as her keeping from marying or having a child by any man .. & as to my Mother that brought me into this world she is to have a maintenance for her estate that was left by her husband which was in WILLIAM & RICHARD KENTS hands .. as to my sister, MARY, that takes care of her Mother and living upon her own means free from anything that is found her Mother therefore let her claim come out of what is in her Mothers hands .. Exers. doe make sail of the same my goods & keep it till my three children come to be of age namly NANCY & SARY & JOHN which then divided equally between them .. hereby ordain JOHN REED & JOHN HAMPTON my Executors .. this 6th day September 1770.

Presence of Samuel x Conner, Mary x Conner, Dugless x Conner

Richard Kent

At a court held .. xixth day August 1771 .. will presented by ELENOR KENT .. admitted to record .. certificate is granted her for obtaining a probate thereof ..

pp. 118-120 We the Subscribers have met at the house of THOMAS DOWDALL decd & have appraised all the estate that was brought to our view .. items valued and totalled, ₤ 179.9.3½ .. includes servant woman named JANE GRIFFIN, another named MARY MURPHEY, a servant man named ROBERT LITTLE MADE BY APPRAISERS CHAS. BROADWATER, EDD. DULIN, JAS. WREN ..

At a court held .. xixth day August 1771 .. inventory returned and ordered to be recorded.

p. We the Subscribers have inventoried & appraised the Estate of
120 GEORGE DARRELL decd .. six items listed with value and totalled, Ł 89.0.6, with notation sorrel horse sold by Capt Darrell to Mr. JOHN GUNNELL for sum of Ten pounds Virginia currency which horse was sold before the appraisement .. made by appraisers THOMAS TRIPLETT, HUMPHREY PEAKE, ABEDNEGO ADAMS.

At a court held .. xxth day August 1771 .. inventory returned & ordered to be recorded.

pp. We whose name is under written have appraised all the Estate of
121- JOHN DOGAN deceased that was presented to our view .. items valued
122 but not totalled .. made by appraisers EDWARD FORD, WILLIAM SIMPSON, MOSES SIMPSON ..

At a court held .. 16th September 1771 .. inventory returned and ordered to be recorded.

pp. Fairfax County September ye 12 1771 a inventory of JOSEPH EARP
122- deceased Estate vallowed by us the Subscribers CHARLES CRAIG, NATHAN
123 FRIZEL & NELSON REED .. items valued and totalled, Ł 81.19.8, which includes ready cash of Ł 41.0.8 ..

At a court held .. 17th September 1771 .. inventory returned and ordered to be recorded.

pp. Will of HANNAH JOHNSTON. I HANNAH JOHNSTON of Fairfax County ..
123- give and bequeath to my son, SAML. JOHNSTON, one young horse & one
124 oval table, one large gun & my hand mill .. to my son, JOHN JOHNSTON, if ever he should return to Fairfax County, Ten pounds currt. money .. unto my Daughter, TAMER SIMPSON .. (dishware and chairs) .. unto my Daughter, FRANCIS CLEAVLAND, her choice of three head of cattle & five pounds current money .. unto my Daughter, ANN THOMPSON, one grey horse and one cow & calf .. unto my Daughter, SUSANNAH JOHNSTON, one negro girl I bought from my son, JOHN JOHNSTON, also one negro woman, one negro boy, one new feather bed and furniture which I have made since the death of my husband .. also a suit of curtains .. (other items) .. unto my Daughter, HANNAH JOHNSTON, one negro woman and Forty pounds current money of Virginia .. (other items) .. residue of my estate to be equally divided between my Daughters, SUSANNAH and HANNAH JOHNSON .. appoint my loving Daughters, SUSANNAH JOHNSTON and HANNAH JOHNSTON, and THOMAS TRIPLETT to be my Executors .. this 8th day of July 1771 ..

Test Samuel Halley,
Barbara x Halley, Stepen x Donaldson

Hannah x Johnston

At a court held .. 17th September 1771 .. will presented by SUSANNAH JOHNSTON and HANNAH JOHNSTON .. same being proved by BARBARY HALLEY and STEPHEN DONALDSON .. admitted to record .. certificate is granted them for obtaining a probate thereof.

pp. Will of THOMAS LEWIS. I THOMAS LEWIS SENIOR of county of Fairfax
124- .. leave to my loving wife, ELIZABETH LEWIS, one third part of my Es-
125 tate during her natural life and after her decease to be equally divided betwixt my ten children, Vizt. THOMAS, JAMES, WILLIAM, HENRY, JOHN, ANN, SARAH, JANE, FRANCIS, WINIFRED LEWISES, and for the other part after the one third taken out .. my will it be equally divided betwixt THOMAS LEWIS, JAMES LEWIS, WM. LEWIS, HENRY LEWIS, JOHN LEWIS, ANN LEWIS, SARAH LEWIS, JANE LEWIS, FRANS. LEWIS and WINEFRED LEWIS .. those not of age their estates to be left in care of THOMAS & JAMES LEWIS to pay .. appoint my loving wife, ELIZABETH LEWIS, THOS. LEWIS,

JAMES LEWIS and WINIFRED LEWIS my Executors .. this 15th day of July 1771 ..

Presence of Elija. Williams, Thomas x Lewis
John Barrett, Saml. x Weaden

At a court held .. 17th September 1771 .. will presented by ELIZABETH LEWIS .. admitted to record .. certificate is granted her for obtaining a probate thereof ..

pp. 125-127 Estate of WILLIAM BERKLEY Deced. DR. To Hector Ross, Gent., Thomas Connel, John Mercer, Benjamin Sebastian, Robert Sandford, Capt. William Ellzey, Hugh West, Edward Payne, John Monk, Doctr. James Nesbett, Majr. Peter Wagener, Charles Binns, Benja. Berkley, Benjamin Grayson, Vincent Lewis, Mary Cleaveland, Joseph Stephens, William Bayly, William Berkley Junr. for his legacy, Catharine Connel for her legacy, Jane Burres for her legacy, Benjamin Berkley for his legacy, charge and trouble of administration (£ 15). Contra. By James Deneale, Lashwell Grasty, Marmaduke Beckwith, William Turner, Joseph Lewis, Elizabeth Berkley, Ann Berkley, by wages yearned by Frank paid and his price when sold to Wm. Berkley, Jane Burross and Benja. Berkley.

At a court held .. 19th September 1771 .. BENJAMIN MASON, Executor of the last will and testament of WILLIAM BERKLEY deced exhibited this account .. is allowed and ordered to be recorded.

pp. 127-128 We the Subscribers have appraised the Estate of THOMAS LEWIS Deced in current money .. items valued and totalled, £ 259.13.2½ .. made by appraisers W. PAYNE JR., JOHN DULIN, PHILIP x GRIMES.

At a court held .. 13th November 1771 .. This inventory was returned and ordered to be recorded.

p. 129 We the Subscribers have Inventory'd and appraised the Estate of EWELL VOILETT deced .. items valued and totalled, £ 163.7.9, of which 100 pounds was appraisal of a negro man and a negro woman .. made by appraisers THOMAS TRIPLETT, HUMPHREY PEAKE, JOSEPH CASH.

At a court held .. 18th November 1771 .. inventory returned and ordered to be recorded.

p. 129 We the Subscribers being first sworn before Capt EDWARD PAYNE, Gent. .. have appraised the Estate of GREENBURY PINKSTONE deced in current money .. nine items valued and totalled, £ 14.9.7½ .. made by appraisers ELIJA. WILLIAMS, JNO. TILLETT, GEORGE TILLETT, May 17th 1771 ..

At a court held .. 17th March 1772 .. inventory returned and ordered to be recorded.

pp. 130-131 We the Subscribers being first sworn before CHARLES BROADWATER, Gent. have met at the house of the late BENJA. SEBASTIAN Deced and have appraised all his Estate that was brought to our view .. items valued and totalled, £ 581.3.1½ .. shows JANE MORRISON 11 months servitude, JAMES SIMMONS an orphan, MICHAEL HOOPER 3 days servitude, JOSEPH WHITE 6 months servitude, SARAH MALLARD 9 months servitude .. made by appraisers W. PAYNE JR., BENJA. MOODY, ED. DULIN.

At a court held .. 18th May 1772 .. inventory returned and ordered to be recorded.

pp. 132-134 We the Subscribers did meet and appraise all the Estate of HANNAH JOHNSTON deceased as was brought to our view .. items valued and totalled, £ 70.9.3 .. made by appraisers HUMPHREY PEAKE, WM. TRIPLETT, ABEDNEGO ADAMS.

At a court held .. 18th May 1772 .. inventory returned and ordered to be recorded.

pp. 134-136 Will of DANIEL FRENCH. I DANIEL FRENCH of Fairfax County being sick .. give and devise unto my dear wife, PENELOPE, my Mansion House and dwelling plantation with all the lands thereto belonging and adjoining, that is to say, all my land in Matthews patent, also a tract of land taken up and patented by my deceased Father and two tracts of land I purchased one of NICHOLAS RAGAN the other of EDWARD BLACKBURN .. also all my lands upon and above the Mouth of Dogues Creek which I purchased of the Executors of RICHARD OSBORN Deced, of the Executors of DOCTOR ARBUTHNOT deced, of JOHN MANLEY deced and of JOHN POSEY .. also all my slaves .. desire my friend, COLONEL GEORGE MASON, to accept the sum of fifty pounds as a small testimony of my regard for him; unto Mr. HUGH FRENCH who now liveth with me the sum of fifty pounds; unto my neice, Mrs. SARAH TRIPLETT, wife of Mr. THOMAS TRIPLETT, a negro boy now at Mr. HUMPHREY PEAKES; unto my wifes Brother, Mr. HARRISON MANLEY, all the slaves and other estate now in possession of his mother, Mrs. Manley, to which I now have or may upon the death of Mrs. Manley have any Right or title .. direct my Executors to purchase with the first profits of my estate two slaves for my brother in law, MR. TOWNSEND DADE .. and whereas I am at this time ingaged as an undertaker in Building a church for Truro Parish, it is my will that said church be built & completed .. give my wearing apparel unto JOHN FRENCH who formerly lived at my Quarter in London (Loudoun) .. my silver watch to my nephew, Mr. FRENCH STROTHER .. unto WILLIAM SPENCER the sum of Forty shillings a year during his life to be laid out every year in Clothes by my Executors .. unto my only Daughter, ELIZABETH, all my lands in the County of Prince William, Fairfax and Louden .. not before disposed of .. and all lands and slaves and other Estate I have herein devised unto my wife .. after my said wifes Decease .. appoint my dear wife, PENELOPE, Executrix and my friend, COLONEL GEORGE MASON, Executor .. this 20th day of May 1771.

Presence of Wm. Rumney,
Platt Townsend, Townsend Dade Junr.
Thomas Triplett

Dan: French

At a court held .. xixth May 1772 .. will presented by PENELOPE FRENCH and GEORGE MASON .. admitted to record .. certificate is granted them for obtaining a probate thereof ..

pp. 136-137 Will of EDWARD RIGDON. I EDWARD RIGDON of Town of Alexandria in Fairfax County, Joiner, being sick .. will and devise that my apprentice Boy, ROBERT MILLS, shall serve my son, THOMAS RIGDON, the residue of the time he has to serve at the trade of a Joiner .. profits from his labor shall be for sole benefit of my son .. also give my son, THOMAS RIGDON, the sum of Five pounds Virginia currency in full satisfaction of every claim he may have against any part of my estate .. bequeath unto my wife, ELIZABETH RIGDEN .. all the rest of my estate .. and do make her sole Executor .. this 22nd day April 1772.

Witness: Rob. H: Harrison,
Rcd: Harrison, Joseph H: Harrison

Edward Rigden

At a court held .. xixth May 1772 .. will presented by ELIZABETH RIGDEN .. admitted to record ..

pp. 137-138 1766. Estate of JOHN BALL Deceased. Dr. Funeral expenses to be paid Mr. Henry Riddle, paid John Hurst, William Templeman, Mr. William Payne, William Gardner, John Rhodes, Capt. Sampson Darrell, Mr. Williams Adams, Mr. James Muir, John Ratcliff, Mr. Daniel French, John Bowling, Joseph Thompson, Joseph Moxley appraisers fee, James Green, John Frizzell, Francis Summers, Mr. John Minor, John Bowlings, Capt. John Dalton, William Ellzey, Robert Adams, Thomas Shaw, paid Robt. Harrison on account of William Payne junr. CR. Debt due of Thomas Odaniel, of Daniel Junning, of Francis Watson, James Thomas, Nathan Hugs, Benjamin Williams, Sime Bowling, Alexander Williams, Silvester Adams, John Alexander for Jno. Watson, John Williams, George Ross .. Errors Excepted Moses Ball, Exr.

At a court held .. xxth May 1772 .. MOSES BALL Executor of JOHN BALL deceased exhibited this account .. is allowed and ordered to be recorded.

p. 139 Sep. ye 28: 1771. A Bill of Inventory and ye appraise of goods and chattles working tools utensils house furniture and all thereto belonging to RICHARD KENT, deceased .. items valued and totalled, £ 54.4.9 .. given 28th day of Septr. 1771 by appraisers WILLIAM SIMPSON, JOSEPH JACOBS SENR., JOHN REID.

At a court held .. 17th August 1772 .. inventory returned and ordered to be recorded.

pp. 139-141 June ye 9, 1772 apraisment of ye Estate of EDWARD RIGDONS B(y) THOS. FLEMING, RICHARD LAKE, ROGER CHEW and THOMAS BROWNLY ..items valued and totalled .. £ 126.0.8 ..

At a court held .. 19th August 1772 .. inventory returned and ordered to be recorded.

pp. 141-142 Know all men .. we ALEXANDER HENDERSON, WILLIAM GRAYSON and ROBERT HANSON HARRISON are held and firmly bound unto JOHN WEST, GEORGE MASON, JOHN CARLYLE, BRYAN FAIRFAX and GEO: WASHINGTON, Gent., Justices of the county court of Fairfax .. in the sum of Five hundred pounds Virginia currency .. 23rd September 1772. Whereas above bound ALEXANDER HENDERSON is appointed administrator of all the goods and chattles .. which were of PAUL TURLEY deceased untill an appeal from the judgment of the county court of Fairfax concerning the last will and testament of PAUL TURLEY shall be determined .. Now the condition of the above obligation .. if ALEXANDER HENDERSON do make a true and perfect inventory of said deceased .. above obligation to be void ..
Witness: Pet. Wagener Junr. Alex: Henderson
(No recording date shown.) Will: Grayson Robt. H. Harrison

pp. 142-144 Inventory of the Est. of Mr. WILLIAM CLIFTON deceased .. items valued and totalled, £ 233.9.10½ .. made by appraisers THOMAS TRIPLETT, JOHN WEST, WM. TRIPLETT, HUMPHREY PEAKE.

At a court held .. 19th November 1772 .. inventory returned and ordered to be recorded.

pp. 144-147 An inventory of the Estate of the late THOMAS COLVILL deceas'd .. items valued but not totalled .. made by appraisers JOHN WEST, THOS. SHAW, ARCHD. SANFORD.

At a court held .. 21st December 1772 .. inventory returned and ordered to be recorded.

pp. 148-149 Will of FRANCES COLVILL. I FRANCIS COLVILL, widow of THOMAS COLVILL Gent. deceased .. give and bequeath unto SARAH BERNARD Five pounds for a ring; unto CATHARINE WEST the half dozen Silver Table Spoons, also one half of my bedding, one half of my china, my close stool chair, my Scarlett gown, a covered basket and whatever shall be in the upper drawer of the case of drawers in my bed chamber; unto JOHN WEST JUNR. Hogarths Prints; unto Doctor RUMNEY a mare colt now in his possession; unto ELIZABETH RAMSAY my Spinnet now in her possession; unto my nephew BENJAMIN MOODY, all the residue of my estate desiring him to take care of negro Moll for my sake and do hereby appoint said BENJAMIN MOODY my Executor .. I desire no inventory of my estate may be made nor any Funeral Sermon .. this 29th day March 1772.

Presence John Rhodes,
Richard Lake
Fras. Colvill

At a court held .. 16th March 1773 .. will presented by BENJAMIN MOODY .. admitted to record .. certificate is granted him for obtaining a probate thereof ..

pp. 149-151 Will of HENRY MOORE. I HENRY MOORE of Town of Colchester in county of Fairfax being not in bodily health .. will and Impower my Executors .. to sell my household furniture, stocks of horses, cattle, Hogs and sheep, Plantation utensils and all other my personal estate (except my slaves) and apply purchase money to payment of my debts .. also to sell my lands in province of Maryland .. applied to a debt due from my son, CLEON, to WILLIAM BALMAIN of Alexandria, Merchant, and likewise in payment for two lotts in town of Colchester contracted for by myself one with Mr. CUMBERLAND WILLSON for my son, CLEON, and the other with Mr. WILLIAM TEMPLEMAN for my son, CATO .. any overplus of sums for sales .. I give to my four daughters to be equally divided amongst them. To my four daughters, all my slaves .. provided Mr. GEORGE SUMMERS who married my daughter, SUSANNA, shall return the Negroes, stock and other estate received from me with my said Daughter into the general appraisement .. if he refuses I give (overplus, etc.) to my three daughters, SARAH, JANE KING and ANN PINNER, to be divided amongst them and do utterly exclude my daughter, SUSANNA SUMMERS, from any part .. give to my son, CLEON, all that lott of land in Town of Colchester purchased of Mr. ALEXANDER HENDERSON and whereon I now live .. to my son, CATO, all my tract of land in county of Frederick he paying my son, CLEON, Two hundred pounds current money at four annual payments of Fifty pounds each .. Impower my Executors and request them (if they can) to agree with my wife for any sum of money which they may think reasonable to be paid her in lieu of her Dower in my slaves .. give to Mrs. HANNAH BRENT, wife of Mr. WILLIAM BRENT, of Dumfries the sum of Eight pounds current money, to her Brother, Mr. THOMAS NEALE, the like sum .. appoint my friends, HECTOR ROSS and ALEXANDER HENDERSON Gentlemen and my son, CLEON MOORE, Executors .. this 17th day May 1772 ..

Presence of Wm. Courts, Hen: Moore
Mary Courts, William Hamilton,
John Davidson, Allen Macdonald, Jas. Ratdray (also Rattray)

At a court held .. xixth April 1773 .. will presented by Executors .. admitted to record .. certificate is granted them for obtaining a probate thereof ..

p. 152 September Court 1772. We the Subscribers have valued and appraised all the Estate of PRISCILLA SEBASTIAN decd that has been presented to our view this 28th day of November 1772 .. three items listed with value of £ 13.0.0 .. also sale of three items with value of £15.10.1 .. made by appraisers WILLIAM WRENN, JOHN WRENN, JARRET x TRAMMELL.

At a court held .. 19th April 1773 .. inventory returned and ordered to be recorded.

pp. 152-153 Will of EDWARD VILET. I EDWARD VILET of Fairfax County being sick .. give unto my loving wife, ELENOR VIOLET, all my Estate .. except what land I hold above the road that leads from Colchester to Alexandria upon the west side of piney Run which land I some time agoe sold to Mr. WILLIAM TRIPLETT for Twenty shillings per acre and have received Three pounds in part of pay for said land which land I never made a deed to said TRIPLETT for .. my desire he have such deed .. I desire my loving wife, ELENOR VILET, and my grandson, WM. VILIT. be Executors .. this 13th day October 1772.

Teste Sibyl x Vilit, Edward x Vilit
Mary x Kirk, Susan x Vilit

At a court held .. 17th May 1773 .. will presented by ELEANOR VIOLET and WILLIAM VIOLET .. admitted to record .. certificate is granted them for obtaining a probate thereof ..

pp. 153-154 Will of THOMAS CARSON. I THOMAS CARSON of Town of Alexandria being sick .. Whereas the said THOMAS CARSON and JAMES MUIR on the first day of May 1772 Enter'd into the following Articles of Copartnership, Viz. Memorandum May the 1st 1772 That Thomas Carson and James Muir entered into Joint partnership each to advance 350 pounds currency for the term of three years and renewable then if agreeable to both and that in case either of them die before the Expiration that the Survivor partner should take an inventory of the goods on hand and after all the debts due from us jointly are paid the Ballance should be remitted to those to whom the same should be left .. Now the said Thomas Carson do hereby ratifie the said Articles .. order that my Executors shall sell and dispose of in fee simple my part of a lott which I purchased as a Tenant in common with JAMES MUIR for to pay joint debts .. any surplus paid to JOHN CARSON and JENNEL CARSON, my Brother and Sister and to the children of DAVID McNISH to be equally divided .. constitute my Friends, JOHN MUIR and THOMAS KIRKPATRICK of Town of Alexandria Executors .. this 17th day October 1772 ..

Presence James Steuart, Thomas x Carson
Anthy. Ramsay, Robt. H. Harrison

At a court held .. xxith June 1773 .. will proved by oaths of JAMES STEUART and ROBERT HANSON HARRISON .. which is admitted to record ..

pp. 154-155 On margin. "Ded. to JOHN PIPER per order of Mr. R. BOGGESS this 25 day of Mch 1774."

We the Subscribers having inventoried and appraised all the Estate of Mr. ROBERT BOGGESS deced that was presented to our view & areas .. items valued and totalled, £ 50.5.1 .. made by appraisers JOHN BARRY, WILLIAM REARDON, H. MANLEY.

At a court held .. xxiii June 1773 .. inventory returned and ordered to be recorded.

p. We the Subscribers have appraised the Estate of MARGARETT HAMPTON
156 Deceased .. items valued and totalled, £ 21.4.3 .. made by appraisers BENJAMIN KING, RICHARD KENT, JOHN REED.
At a court held .. xxth July 1773 .. inventory returned and ordered to be recorded.

pp. On margin. "23d Aug 1773 dd A. Henderson Exr"
156- DR. Estate of MARGT. HAMPTON Decd with ALEXR. HENDERSON, admr. ..
158 To the Constable for serving two warrants on Conner & Harraway .. to Prince William County Clerks fees, to Prince William County Sheriffs fees, to MARY HAMPTON for Gilbert Rolands acct., to Pierce Bayly for a debt due to Capt. William Bayliss. CR. Cash received from Richard Kent, from S. Hornbuckle, THOMAS HAMPTON, HENRY HAMPTON, Patrick Conner, JOHN HAMPTON for Merryman Harroway from William Bird, Mordecai Kelly ..
At a court held .. xxth July 1773 .. ALEXANDER HENDERSON administrator of MARGARET HAMPTON deceased exhibited this account .. is allowed and ordered to be recorded.

pp. On margin. "23d August 1773 dd A. Henderson Exr."
158- We the Subscribers being first sworn before EDWARD PAYNE, Gent.
159 having met at the Plantation of MRS. JANE TURLEY deceased and have appraised all the said goods and chattles rendered to our view in current money .. items valued and totalled, £ 209.0.0½ .. mentions large Bible .. made by appraisers WILLIAM SIMPSON, THOS. FORD, THOMAS LUCAS.
At a court held .. xxth July 1773 .. inventory returned and ordered to be recorded.

pp. On margin. "1773 August 23d dd A. Henderson Exr."
159- Acct. of Sales of Estate of JANE TURLEY decd in May 1773 .. to
161 Sampson Turley, Edward Payne, William Marbury, John Waller, Sam: Williams, Daniel Neale, William Gardner, Samuel Randolph, George Jones, Thomas Sangster, John Buckhanan, Charles Broadwater, Thomas Ford, Lee Massey, James Foley, James Butler, Elijah Williams, Thomas Lucas, John Tillett .. amount of sales, £ 94.19.11½ ..
At a court held .. xxth July 1773 .. ALEXANDER HENDERSON and JOHN TILLETT, Executors of JANE TURLEY deceased exhibited to the Court .. account of sales .. ordered to be recorded.

pp. On margin. "1773 August 23d dd A. Henderson Exr."
161- DR. The Estate of Mrs. JEAN TURLEY deceased with ALEXANDER HENDER-
166 SON and JOHN TILLETT, Executors .. to Pierce Bayly Sheriff for publick dues, to Jean Sheat, to Hargis King, Thomas Ford, Doctor George, Richard Simpson, Thomas Sangster, Edward Payne, Elijah Williams, William Gardner, John Turley, Revd. Lee Massey preaching a funeral sermon, William Grayson, Sampson Turley. CR. Thomas Lucas, George Tillett, James Foley, George Jones, James Stewart, Alexandria, Daniel Neale, John Waller security for Butler interest, Thomas Montgomery (1769) one negro girl to SAMPSON TURLEY for his wife, MARTHA, to JAMES LEWIN GIBBS for his wife, JEAN, to SAMPSON for his several children for HENRIETTA TURLEY, for MARTHA TURLEY, for ANN TURLEY, for JOHN TURLEY 1 large Bible, for GILES TURLEY, to JOHN WALDEN for his wife, MARY, to ditto for his son, JOHN, to John Tillett, to Elijah Connell 20/ currency .. she lives in Carolina therefore this cannot be got to her hands ..

At a court held .. xxth July 1773 .. ALEXANDER HENDERSON and JOHN TILLETT, Executors of JEAN TURLEY deced exhibited this account .. is approved of and JOHN TURLEY the residuary legatee having come into Court and acknowledged his approbation of the said account and that he is indebted to the said Executors the sum of Two pounds Eleven shillings and Three pence the said account is allowed and ordered to be recorded .. and said Executors having delivered to SAMPSON TURLEY sundry specific Legacies devised by the decedent to HENRIETTA TURLEY, MARTHA TURLEY, ANN TURLEY, JOHN TURLEY and GILES TURLEY .. also a legacee to JOHN WALDEN an infant .. appears to the Court Executors have fully discharged their duty.

pp. 166-168 By Order directing us to appraise the Estate of JOSEPH THOMPSON decd we made the following appraisement Decr. 31, 1772 .. items valued and totalled, ₤ 191.10.0½ .. made by appraisers JOHN DALTON, JOHN MUIR, JONATHAN HALL.

At a court held .. 21st July 1773 .. inventory returned and ordered to be recorded.

pp. 168-175 On margin. "Dd Colo. Mason"

Inventory and Appraisement Estate Mr. DANIEL FRENCH decd at his Mansion House and Dogues Creek Quarter in Fairfax County .. one silver watch bequeathed to FRENCH STROTHER, wearing apparel bequeathed to JOHN FRENCH, one negro bequeathed to Mrs. TRIPLETT, 40 other negroes other items valued and totalled, ₤ 2317.16.7 .. made 31st August 1772 by appraisers HUMPHREY PEAKE, SAMPSON DARRELL, THOS. MONROE.

Inventory and Appraisement of the Estate of Mr. DANIEL FRENCH decd at his Quarter on Pohick Run at the new Church that is building at Pohick and in Town of Colchester in Fairfax County .. shows 26 negroes besides one child .. items valued and totalled ₤ 1525.10.6 .. made by same appraisers.

Inventory and Appraisement of the Estate of Mr. DANIEL FRENCH decd at his Quarter near the Falls Church in Fairfax County .. shows 17 negroes besides four children .. items valued and totalled, ₤ 959.11.6 .. given 4th day December 1772 by appraisers CHAS. BROADWATER, WM. PAYNE JR., JAMES WREN.

Inventory and Appraisement of Estate of Mr. DANIEL FRENCH decd in Loudoun County .. shows 28 negroes .. items valued and totalled, ₤ 1358.18.3 .. given 4th day December 1772 by appraisers LEVEN POWELL, SIMON HANCOCK, WM. BRONAUGH.

Inventory and Appraisement of Estate of Mr. DANIEL FRENCH decd in Prince William County .. shows 12 negroes .. items valued and totalled, ₤ 302.3.0, given 17th day March 1772 by JOHN TYLER, JOHN BRETT, JOHN HOOE.

Return combines inventores showing total appraised value of the five inventories of ₤ 6963.19.10. Returned by GEORGE MASON, acting Executor.

At a court held .. xxth September 1773 .. inventorys and appraisements returned and ordered to be recorded.

pp. 175-177 Will of WILLIAM THOM. I WILLIAM THOM Minister of the Gospel in Town of Alexandria being indisposed in body .. give towards building a Presbyterian Church in Alexandria Fifty pounds Pensylvania money .. give to the REVD. JAMES WILLSON, Minister of the Gospel in new London in Pensylvania Fifty pounds that money and all my printed books; to

JAMES THOM SENIOR of Lancaster County in Pensylvania in that money Fifty pounds; to SARAH TAYLOR, Sister to my late Mother the sum of Fifty pounds Pensylvania money; to JOHN HOMES or HOMES JUNR. of Carlisle in Pensylvania all my wearing apparel, my watch, my horse, saddle and bridle; to MARGARET COCKBURN now in Alexandria Ten pounds Pens. money; to SARAH TAYLOR all the rest of my mothers wearing apparrel; to JAMES HENDRICKS of Alexandria a merchant my chest of Drawers; to WILLIAM RAMSAY of Alexandria my Burrian or Desk; to RICHARD ARRELL of Alexa. my tea table; that my Executors give freedom from servitude my servant woman HANNAH BROWN; residue of my estate equally divided between JAMES THOM and SARAH TAYLOR .. appoint JAMES HENDRICKS, the REVD. JAMES WILLSON and WILLIAM RAMSAY Executors .. this 6th day August 1773 ..
Presence of James Hunt,
John Carlyle
Wm. Thom

At a court held .. xxth September 1773 .. will presented (by Executors) .. admitted to record .. certificate is granted them for obtaining a probate thereof ..

pp. Will of SAMUEL JOHNSON. I SAMUEL JOHNSON of Fairfax County being
177- sick .. give and bequeath to my beloved daughter, HANNAH JOHNSON,
178 when she comes of age or marries one Negroe girl; to my beloved son, VINSON JOHNSON, when he comes of age one Negroe girl; to my beloved wife, CATHERINA JOHNSON, all the rest of my estate .. after her decease what remains to be equally divided among all my children .. appoint my beloved wife, CATHERINA JOHNSON, my Executrix jointly with my good friend, EPHERIM DICKEN .. this 19th day December 1772.
Presence of John x Spinks,
Abraham x Beach, James Connell
Sam'l. Johnson

At a court held .. xxth September 1773 .. will presented by Executor and Executrix .. admitted to record .. a certificate is granted them for obtaining a probate thereof ..

pp. On margin. "dd Alex Henderson 14th Decr. 1773"
178- An Inventory and Appraisement of such of the personal estate and
184 slaves of HENRY MOORE deceased as are presented to our view in Fairfax County this 23rd day April 1773 .. items valued and totalled, £ 469.3.3 .. made by appraisers LEE MASSEY, W. COURTS, W. THOMPSON. Sworn before H. ROSS.

An Inventory and Appraisement of the personal estate and slaves of HENRY MOORE in county of Loudoun .. 30th day April 1773 .. items valued and totalled, £ 303.4.9 .. made by appraisers JAS. LANE, JOHN ORR, SAML. LOVE. Sworn 30th April 1773 before GEO. SUMMERS.

An Inventory and appraisement Est of HENRY MOORE .. 28th April 1773 in county of Berkley .. items valued and totalled, £ 566.4.9, appraised by WILLIAM LITTLE, HUGH STEPHENSON, RICHD. STEPHENSON .. sworn 28th April 1773 before THOS. RUTHERFORD.

Report combines three inventories to show total appraised value of £ 1338.12.9 ..

At a court held .. 18th October 1773 .. These inventories and appraisements returned and ordered to be recorded.

pp. We the Subscribers have appraised the Estate of THOMAS WEST decd
184- .. items valued and totalled, £ 124.19.11 .. made by appraisers MOSES
185 SIMPSON, WILLIAM SIMPSON, THOS. FORD, SAMUEL LITTLEJOHN ..

At a court held .. 18th October 1773 .. inventory returned and ordered to be recorded.

pp. 185-186 An Inventory of the Estate of ABRAHAM WRIGHT decd taken this 8th day of August 1773 .. items valued and totalled, £ 61.4.6 .. made by appraisers JOHN WEST JUNR., GERD. x BOWLING, PETER WISE.

At a court held .. 19th October 1773 .. inventory returned and ordered to be recorded.

pp. 186-187 We whose names are under written being first legaly sworn did on the 13 day November appraise and Inventory the Estate of ABSOLOM THRIFT Deced all such as come to our view .. items valued and totalled, £ 81.12.4 .. made by appraisers JOHN JACKSON JUNER., JOHN SHORTRIDGE, DANIEL JENKINS.

At a court held .. 15th November 1773 .. inventory returned and ordered to be recorded.

pp. 187-188 Will of MICHAEL REAGAN. I MICHAEL REAGAN of Fairfax County being sick and weak in Body .. give and bequeath unto my eldest son, NICHOLAS REAGAN, a Feather bed and furniture, likewise Four hundred acres of land out of this track I now live on .. in default of heirs to be equally divided amongst the rest of my children that is to say SARAH REAGAN which is the wife of WM. TOLBERT, to ANN REAGAN, CONSTANT REAGAN and MILDRED REAGAN .. (to each unmarried daughter a feather bed and furniture) .. unto CONSTANT REAGAN and MILDRED REAGAN the remainder of the track of land to be equally divided between them both allso three tracks of land at the new Church whereon THOS. CRAFFORD lives to be delivered to them at age of Eighteen or at the day of marriage .. in default to be returned to my well beloved son, NICHOLAS REAGAN .. unto my son, MICHAEL REAGAN, one shilling sterling in Debaring him of any claim Rite or title to any part of my Estate having given him more already than his part of the Estate would come to. I give to MARGETT ASHFORD a suit of Close in Debaring her (same as in Michael) ..I give unto my well beloved wife, REBECKAH REAGAN, all the rest of my estate during her natural life including this Plantation where I now lives on .. after her decease to dispose of the Estate as she thinks proper among the children. It is my will that she will give Eaqual part with the rest and to my granddaughter, SARAH REAGAN, the daughter of PETER REAGAN, to be paid at Eighteen or at the day of marriage .. appoint my well beloved wife, REBEKAH REAGAN, and my son, NICHOLAS REAGAN, to be Executors .. this 25th day March 1758 (sic).

Presence William Wren, Michaell Reagan

Spence Neal, Nicholas Reagan

At a court held .. 15th November 1773 .. will presented by NICHOLAS REAGAN .. proved by oaths of WILLIAM WREN and NICHOLAS REAGAN and is admitted to record .. certificate is granted him for obtaining a probate thereof .. At a court held .. xxth November 1776 .. WILLIAM WREN made oath that SPENCE NEALE subscribed this will in his presence at the request of MICHAEL REAGAN the Testator which is ordered to be certified ..

p. 188 Will of GILBERT SIMPSON. I GILBERT SIMSON of Fairfax County being weak of body .. give and bequeath to my daughter, VALINDA SIMSON, my best bed and furniture .. to my granddaughter, KESSIAH, my next best bed and furniture. I give to my son, JOHN SIMSON, as much of my Estate as shall be of the Vallew of a bed and furniture .. to my loving wife, ELIZABETH SIMSON, all the rest of my Estate during her life, also it is my will that if the Stock be too Burdensum to her that then she

will sell or dispose of to her children as she thinks fit .. at the death of my wife, my whole estate be Equally divided amongst my whole children .. my will that my son, GILBERT SIMPSON, and my wife be Executors .. this 7th day July 1773.
Presence Sampson Darrell, Gilbert Simpson
Josias x Payne
At a court held .. 17th November 1773 .. will presented by (Executors) .. admitted to record .. certificate is granted them for obtaining a probate thereof ..

p. 1767. DR. Estate of ALEXANDER MILLS in account with RHODHAM
189 SIMPSON and his wife, Executors .. cash paid Elijah Williams; James Nisbett; John Griffin; John Tillett, Baxter Simpson .. total £ 6.4.9.
1769. DR. The Estate of ALEXANDER MILLS in account with RHODHAM SIMPSON and ANN, his wife .. Boarding 3 children two years to go to school @ £ 6 each; payments made by Thomas Parkins for the Estate .. £ 42.4.9.
Contra. Amount of inventory except the slave; part wages for the slave for 3 years two thirds .. £ 60.4.3.
At a court held .. 17th Novr. 1773 .. RHODHAM SIMPSON who intermarried with AN PERKINS, wife of THOMAS PERKINS Decd, Exor. of ALEXANDER MILLS Decd Exhibited this account .. is allowed and ordered to be recorded.

pp. Fairfax. Decmr. 16th 1773. We the Subscribers .. have appraised
189- and Inventoried all the Estate of SAMUEL JOHNSON Deceased as was pre-
190 sented to our view .. items valued and totalled, £ 344.0.8 .. made by appraisers WILLIAM PAYNE, SANFORD RAMEY, JOSEPH POWELL.
At a court held .. xxith February 1774 .. inventory and appraisement returned and ordered to be recorded.

pp. December 1771. A Second Appraisement of the Estate of BENJAMIN
190- SEBASTIAN .. items valued and totalled, £ 25.1.0 (consists of apprai-
191 sal of a number of pigs and a parcel of old Law Books) .. made by appraisers WM. PAYNE, JAS. WREN, ED. DULIN, BENJA. MOODY ..
At a court held .. 21st Feby. 1774 .. inventory returned and ordered to be recorded.

p. We the Subscribers being appointed and first sworn before EDWARD
191 PAYNE, Gent. .. have appraised and Inventoried the Estate of GEORGE MARTIN Deceased in current money .. items valued and totalled, £ 85.18.11½ .. made by appraisers THOS. FORD, ELIJA. WILLIAMS.
At a court held .. xxith February 1774 .. inventory returned and ordered to be recorded.

pp. We the Subscribers being appointed appraisers of the Estate of
191- DAVID GORDAN Deceased make the following appraisement Viz. October 22,
193 1773 .. items valued and totalled, £ 47.16.8½ .. includes a Silver watch, 1 pr. Silver shoe and knee buckles .. made by appraisers JOHN LOMAX, JOHN SHAW, THO. LOGAN.
At a court held .. 23d March 1774 .. inventory returned and ordered to be recorded ..

pp. Sales of DAVID GORDONS Estate October the 30, 1773 .. sold to
193- Osborn Talbot; William Allison; Robert Adam; John Dalton; Mich. McClay;
194 Thomas Moxley; John Stuart; Thomas Dayly; Antho. Hedrick; Igns. McFarlain; John Savage; Jane Gordan, John Harper, Levy Talbot, Benja.

Stuart, Danl. Haley, John Shaw . . John Dalton, admr. .. amount of sale, £ 73.12.11½ ..
At a court held .. 23rd March 1774 .. Account of Sales returned and ordered to be recorded.

pp. Will of BENONI KENT. The fifth day of August 1772, I BENONI KENT
194- of Fairfax County an Parish of Truro, Planter, being sick .. give and
195 bequeath to JEAN my Dearly Beloved wife the one third part of my Estate .. to my beloved Daughter, ANN CARACOE, two cows and two calves with the other things I formerly lent her .. remainder of my Estate be Equally devided between my other Ten children, Viz. JOHN, SAMUEL, DANIEL, THOMAS, SAMPSON and PETER, SUSANNER, MARY, SARAH and ELIZABETH .. MY WILL AND Desire is that my sons Shalt be for their Selves at age of Eighteen years if my wife should think proper to marry, my will is that my estate be Devided at the appraisement as above mentioned .. make my Beloved Son, JOHN KENT, my Executor ..
Presence Jonathan Denty,
Samuel x Clark, Henry x Loyd Benoni x Kent
At a court held .. 24th March 1774 .. will presented by JOHN KENT .. admitted to record .. certificate is granted him for obtaining a probate thereof ..

p. We the Subscribers being first sworn have Inventoryed the Esta.
195 of Mrs. ELIZABETH ASHFORD .. items valued and totalled, £ 92.8.6 .. made by appraisers THOMAS TRIPLETT, ABEDNEGO ADAMS, WM. TRIPLETT.
At a court held .. 16th May 1774 .. inventory returned and ordered to be recorded.

pp. The Estate of Mr. DANIEL FRENCH deced in account with GEORGE MASON,
196- acting Executor and Guardian of his daughter, ELIZABETH .. DR. specific
212 legacies delivered to .. silver watch to FRENCH STROTHER, wearing apparel to JOHN FRENCH, a negro boy to MRS. TRIPLETT (the wife of Mr. THOMAS TRIPLETT), remainder of all the slaves and chattels at the Mansion House and Dogues Creek Quarter Delivered to the decd widow, Mrs. PENELOPE FRENCH, to whom they were bequeathed for her life; all the Slaves and chattels in the Pohick Quarter, new Pohick church and Colchester inventory kept upon the Estate for the decd granddaughter and Heiress, Miss ELIZA. FRENCH; HUGH FRENCH for his Legacy; GEORGE MASON for his Legacy; (1771) my own claim against the Estate; APPOLLOS COOPER for brick work at the Church; Colo. GEORGE WASHINGTON for 32 M shingles for the Church; WM. MELONY for freight of 30,090 shingles from Suffolk; DOCTR. PLATT TOWNSHEND; WILLIAM COURTS; ROBERT BOGGESS for the purchase of 130 acres of land on Pohick agreed by Mr. French in his life time and the Deeds since taken in his Daughter's name; paid for a horse for Mr. THOS. TRIPLETT to ride to the Estate Quarters etc. he being employed to over look them. CR .. lists the inventories at the various locations; NB all that part of the Estate charged per contra kept for the Deceased's Daughter and Heiress, Miss ELIZABETH FRENCH, is now in the possession of her husband, BENJAMIN DULANY Esqr. .. (1771) WM. MELONY for a deficiency of 1910 shingles; Truro Parish for the third payment for the new church, Mr. French having reseived the first two payments in his life time; Mr. JAMES STEWART a set of Exchange pble to HARRY PIPER; cash from Mr. JAMES STEWART per my ordr. to Miss ELIZA. FRENCH; from do to JAMES CONNELLY;

DR. 1771. Cash paid JOHN FLETCHER, ELIAS HOARE, THOMAS DUNAWAY; to HARRY PIPER for flag stone from Mr. DIXON; WM. COPEIN for stone work at the church; GOWING LAMPHIER for Joiners work; WM. CHALK for the workman at the church; JAMES CONNELLY for a Walnutt Coffin in a pine case for the Deceased; FRANCIS POSTON overseer for his share; JAMES SERVIS overseer for his share of crop made in 1770; WILLM. CLEVELAND overseer for his share of crop made in 1770; JAMES ORAM overseer for his share of the crop made in 1770; Mrs. PENELOPE FRENCH for cash paid Mrs. BROMLEY for her attendance at Mr. French's funeral; (1772) JAMES HARDWICH LANE; ROBT. BOGGESS JUNR.; Mr. ROBERT ADAM; WILLIAM CARLIN.

Mr. French died in May 1771 before which he had sold his crop of Tobacco made in 1770 to Mr. JAMES STEWART Mercht. in Alexandria with the goods for the sd Tobo Miss ELIZA. FRENCH'S Slaves were Cloathed and herself and her Quarters furnished with necessarys .. (1772) ROBT. HANSON HARRISON for his Debt due Estate; WM. CULLINSON his rent due for year 1771; THOS. BROOKBANK for do; Mrs. PENELOPE FRENCH for her part of quit rents due for year 1771 being for 2000 acres of land; SAML. JOHNSTON for prizing three light Hhds. in his crop; Messrs. HALL & GILPIN for JAS. FRENCH'S order to me in part of HUGH FRENCH'S Legacy; Mr. CHARLES ALEXANDER his debt to Estate.

DR. To. Mr. Sampson Darrell, James Noland, Michael Reagan, Joseph Moxly, Richard Lake, Charles Turner, Elias Poston, Doctor William Rumney, John Hooe, Jacob Thomas, Newman Matthews, Bernard Sears, Gowing Lamphier, Thos. Lawson, Jeremiah Cullinson, Josias Miles, Wm. Payne, John Ratliff, Benjam. Hatten and Laurence Lewis for labourers wages; James Rhodes, Mr. Dade for preaching a funeral sermon for the Decd last year .. (1772) Thomas Baker, John Reid, William Cullinson, Humphry Peake, Thos. Fleming, Wm. Carr Lane; Thos. Triplett, Edwd. Sprigg, William Cleveland, James Lewis overseer, Reubin Cleveland overseer, Samuel Johnston overseer; Gerard Spinks overseer, Wm. Spencer, William Simpson, Robert Philips; Thos. Simmonds; Alexr. Keith; Alexander Campbell Merchant in Dumfries, Charles Porter.

(1772) .. from Colin Dunlope and son and Companys store in Dumfries .. (1773) Mr. Hector Ross, Wm. Cullinsons rent for 1772; Benjm. Dulany Esqr., two hhds. Tobo received from GEORGE & ISAAC NEWMAN in part payment for their rents; Mr. Alexander Campbell; Thos. Brookbank for rent 1772 .. (1773) None of the crop ever made in 1773 ever came into the hands of G. MASON nor did he receive any of the rents due for the year, MR. DULANY having taken the Estate into his own possession and he even sold the corn that was to spare at the Loudoun Quarter made in 1772 (while the Estate was in G. MASON'S hands) and applied the money to his own use altho he new that G. MASON was at the time largely in advance for the Estate .. there was no wheat made at the Quarters while they were in G. MASON'S hands except at Loudoun Quarter and that was sold to POWELL & HARRISON (who had a considerable demand against the Estate) and is credited by them in their account .. (1774) ROBT. BOGGESS for rent of the Fishery at Belmont for year 1772; ISAAC NEWMAN for balance of his rents for 1771 & 1772; GEORGE NEWMAN do; for sundry materials left when Church was finished; James Hardwich Lane; RICHARD ARRELL for a balla. he owed Mr. French; Mr. G. Mason has not charged commissions upon many Articles on which it is Customary to charge commissions .. he loses about half the Interest upon an Average each year.

JAMES HARDWICH LANE for lodging BERNARD SEARS while he was painting and glazing the church in 1772; 114 nights @ 3d .. paid William Williams; Thos. Kirkpatrick; Robt. Carter Nicholas Esqr.; Townshend Dade for legacy of two negroes; Mr. James Wrenn; accts due Oswald Denniston and Co.

At a court held .. 20th September 1774 .. GEORGE MASON Gent, acting Executor of Estate of DANIEL FRENCH decd and guardian to ELIZABETH, the Decedents Daughter, exhibited this account .. is allowed and ordered to be recorded.

p. 212 We the Subscribers have met together and appraised the Estate of BENONI KENT Deceased .. items valued and totalled, £ 1056.0.6 .. March Court 1774 GRAFTON KIRKE, ED. x SHILTON, THOMAS HARDINGE.

At a court held .. xvth May 1774 .. inventory returned and ordered to be recorded.

pp. 215-216 Will of HARRISON MANLEY. I HARRISON MANLEY of Fairfax County .. give unto my loving wife, MARGT. MANLEY, the use of my whole Estate during her natural life provided she remains a widow .. in case she should marry .. Estate should be Equally divided by my Executors between my wife, MARGRET MANLEY, my son, JOHN MANLEY, my Daughter, SARAH MANLEY, my Daughter, MARY MANLEY and my Daughter, PENELOPE MANLEY .. appoint my loving wife, MARGRET MANLEY, my Brother, WILLIAM TRIPLETT, and my Brother, THOMAS TRIPLETT, and my friend, LUND WASHINGTON, to be Executors .. this 8th day of December 1773.

Presence Penelope French, Hi. Manley
Wm. Rumney, Mary Manley

At a court held .. xvith May 1774 .. will presented .. admitted to record .. certificate is granted (Executors) for obtaining a probate ..

pp. 216-217 Will of ELIZABETH SEBASTIAN. I ELIZABETH SEBASTIAN of Fairfax Parish in county of Fairfax being very sick .. give and bequeath to GEORGE McCORMACK my proportion of land lying in Parish of Fairfax and in Fairfax County which my father devised to be equally divided between my sester, BEHETHLIAM SEBASTIAN and me .. to SARAH McCORMACK, daughter of GEORGE McCORMACK, one bed with all necessary furniture .. give to AMELIA WATSON one bed with all nessary furniture .. to JOHN McCORMACK, son of GEORGE McCORMACK, one silver watch; to SARAH McCORMACK one tea chest with six Silver Tea Spoons and one pair of Silver Tea Tongs .. I give all my pewter and earthenware to be equally divided between SARAH McCORMACK and AMELIA WATSON .. appoint my Friend, GEORGE McCORMACK, my Executor .. this 23d day of Feby. 1773.

Presence John Minor, Elizabeth Sebastian
Ann Minor, Elizabeth x Read

At a court held .. 16th May 1773 .. will presented by GEORGE McCORMACK .. is ordered to be recorded.

p. 217 Estate of RICHD. OSBORN Decd. DR to JOHN KING Exr. (1771). Paid WILLIAM SPENCER in part of a Legacy ..

At a court held .. 16th May 1774 .. JOHN KING Exer. of RICHARD OSBORN Decd Exhibited this account .. is allowed and ordered to be recorded.

pp. 217-218 Estate of PRISSILLIAH SEBASTIAN Deceased by JARRAID TRAMMEL, WILLIAM WREN and JOHN WREN .. (1772) GEORGE McCORMICK admr. paid WILLIAM MUNDAY for making a coffin ..

At a court held .. xxvth day May 1774 .. GEORGE McCORMICK administrator of PRISALLA SEBASTIAN Deceased exhibited this account .. is allowed and ordered to be recorded.

pp. 218-219 Account of the Sale of the Estate of ROBERT BOGGESS Deceased July 16th 1773 .. sale totalled £ 469.8.3 .. no purchasers shown.
At a court held .. xxth May 1774 Account of Sales presented by ROBERT BOGGESS, Admor. and is ordered to be recorded.

pp. 219-220 Estate of ROBERT BOGGESS, Decd .. (1772) DR. Paid GEORGE WEST surveyor; FRANCIS RANDALL .. decedent's bond; balance HENRY THRELKELD'S bond; WILLIAM PAYNE, Gent.; paid JOHN GIBSON the amount of Decedents debt to OSWALD DENNISTON and Company; HECTOR ROSS. Errors Excepted ROBERT BOGGESS Admor.
At a court held .. xxth May 1774 .. account exhibited and ordered to be recorded.

p. 221 Will of MICHAEL COYLE. I MICHAEL COYL of Alexandria Town in Fairfax County, Cordwainer, being sick .. give and bequeath unto my Loving Brother, BENJAMIN COYLE, of Spotsylvania County, Cordwainer, and also unto his eight children, VIDILICET, ELIZABETH, JAMES, KIZZIA, MICHAEL, MARY, BENJAMIN, LUCY and WILLIAM each of then one shilling sterling money of great Britain .. unto my loving wife, MARY, whom I constitute Executrix .. all my Estate and Effects .. this 8th day March 1774.
Presence Peter Robinson,
Thomas Witherinton, Mary x Witherinton Michael Coyle
At a court held .. xxth June 1774 .. will presented by MARY COYL .. admitted to record .. certificate is granted her for obtaining a probate thereof ..

pp. 221-223 Will of PAUL TURLEY. I PAUL TURLEY of county of Fairfax and Parish of Truro being very sick .. give and bequeath unto my son, IGNATIOUS TURLEY, 110 acres of land, it being part of a tract of land bought of THOS. MONK and whereon the said IGNATIOUS TURLY now lives .. on his paying Fifty pounds current money of Virginia within twelve months after this will is in force towards discharging a debt due Mr. ALEXR. HENDERSON, and for the said TURLEY by the above gift above mentioned therewith for him to be content. I give unto my son, JOHN TURLEY, 180 acres of land binding on IGNATIOUS TURLEYS land and the place whereon I now live .. on his paying Fifty pounds current money of Virginia according as before mentioned .. if he should die .. my desire 180 acres should fall to my younger son, PAUL TURLEY .. give to my son, PAUL TURLEY, the House and Orchard on the premises with 110 acres of Land joining thereto .. on his paying Fifty pounds current money of Virginia as before mentioned .. if he should die without heirs, should fall to my son, JOHN TURLEY .. unto my Daughter, ANN IRWIN, Twenty shillings and for her therewith to be content .. unto my Daughter, JANE CHURCH, Twenty shillings and for her therewith to be content .. unto my Daughter, LYDIA VEALE (same) .. unto my Daughter, MONEYEA HAZEL (same) .. untc my Daughter, RACHEL BUCKHANNON (same) .. unto my daughter, HELENE, one Feather bed and furniture to be delivered to her at age of Eighteen years or day of Marriage. I give unto my Daughter, STACEY TURLEY, one negro boy; unto my daughter, ELIZABETH TURLEY, Fifty pounds current money of Virginia to be paid after the decease of my wife, SARAH TURLEY .. unto my daughter, MARY TURLEY, Fifty pounds current money of Virginia to be paid her as before directed and mentioned .. unto my loving wife all the remainder part of my estate .. at her decease to dispose of it as she shall think proper .. appoint

my loving wife, SARAH TURLEY, JOHN TURLEY and my son, PAUL TURLEY, Executors .. this 23rd day March 1772.
Presence Elija. Williams, Paul x Turley
Samuel Tillet, Anne Tillet
At a court held .. 16th June 1772 .. will presented (by Executors) and IGNATIOUS TURLEY the heir at law came into court and took the advantage of being summoned and having contested the validity of the will, the court upon Examination of the Witnesses and heard parties by their counsel are of opinion Will is good and ordered to be recorded from which opinion the said IGNATIOUS TURLEY prays an appeal to the next General Court who with WILLIAM REED acknowledged a Bond for prosecuting the same with Effect.

p. 223 Will of WILLIAM SHAW. I WILLIAM SHAW of the Town of Alexandria in county of Fairfax being sick .. give and devise that part of the Lott I now live on at the Intersection of Royal and Queen street, Easterly with Queen street to the plank fence or partition running Southerly from the said street to the south side of my part of the said Lott .. (further description) .. unto my son, THOMAS SHAW .. the remainder part of my said Lott lying to the Eastward .. unto my two daughters, ISABELL and ELIZABETH .. provided always my wife, ELEANOR, shall have said Lott during her life unless she shall Incline to give Them to the several Devisees before her death. I devise the Lott on which my shop stands on the north side of Queen street unto my wife .. after her death I give same unto my son, WILLIAM SHAW. I appoint my Dear wife, ELEANOR SHAW, my Friends, THOMAS KIRKPATRICK and ROBERT ADAM, Executors .. this 19th day December 1774.
Presence James Connell, Will. Shaw
James Muir, Rob. H. Harrison
At a court held .. January 19th 1775 .. will presented by THOMAS KIRKPATRICK and ROBERT ADAM .. proved .. ordered to be recorded.
At a court held .. 19th June 1775 .. will proved by oaths of ELEANOR SHAW and ROBERT ADAM .. certificate is granted them for obtaining a probate thereof ..

pp. 224-225 Will of JOHN CLARK. I JOHN CLARK of Truro Parish and county of Fairfax being sick .. give unto my loving wife, BARBARY CLARK, the use of all my whole estate .. except two negroes .. and one Feather bed which I give unto my son, JOHN CLARK .. unto my daughter, SARAH PILCHER, one negro girl .. unto my daughter, WINNEY PILCHER, one negro girl .. unto my daughter, ELIZABETH SIMPSON, one negro girl .. unto my daughter, SUSANAH MOORE, a negro girl .. unto my son, JOHN CLARK, two negroes .. and at the decease of his mother the remainder of my estate .. my further will is that there shall be no appraisement or Security given .. appoint my dearly beloved wife, BARBARY CLARK, and also my dear son, JOHN CLARK, Executors .. this 19th day June 1772.
Presence William Turner, John Clark
Mary Ellzey, Sarah Turner
At a court held .. 17th April 1775 .. will presented by BARBARA CLARK and JOHN CLARK .. admitted to record .. certificate is granted them for obtaining a probate thereof ..

p. 225 Will of RICHARD LAKE. I RICHARD LAKE of county of Fairfax being in my perfect senses .. whereas I am indebted to my Sister in law, MARY SAUNDERS, Eighty pounds Virginia currency, my will is she may live in a convenient manner in my House during her life in Satisfaction of said Debt if she chooses so to do .. if she shall choose to receive the Eighty pounds it is my will she not be Intitled to any part of my House .. this 3rd day March 1775.

Presence John Allison, Richd. x Lake
Martha x Kay, John West Junr.

At a court held .. 17th April 1775 .. This Instrument of Writing was proved by oaths of JOHN ALLISON and MARTHA KEY to be the last will and testament of RICHARD LAKE Deceased which is ordered to be recorded.

pp. 225-229 Will of ELIZABETH CLIFTON. I ELIZABETH CLIFTON of Fairfax County, Widow and Relict of WILLIAM CLIFTON, late of same county, deceased, being in perfect sense .. give and bequeath unto my daughter, ANN SLAUGHTER, one tract of land lying in Stafford County and also a tract of land lying in Fairfax County containing by pattent 650 acres .. after the death of my daughter, ANN SLAUGHTER, one moiety of said tract of land lying in Fairfax County unto my granddaughter, ELIZABETH BRENT SLAUGHTER .. in default of heirs .. said moiety to my granddaughter, ELEANOR CLIFTON SLAUGHTER .. in default of heirs to the next child that may be born of my daughter, ANN SLAUGHTER .. default to my Cousen, HENRY BRENT .. (then) ANN BRENT; other moiety after death of my daughter, ANN SLAUGHTER, to my granddaughter, ELEANOR CLIFTON SLAUGHTER .. (enumerates descent in default of heirs) .. I give and bequeath after the death of my daughter, ANN SLAUGHTER, one moiety of the land I have in Stafford County to my granddaughter, ELIZABETH BRENT SLAUGHTER .. (enumerates descent including to ROBERT BRENT, son of ROBERT, the son of GEORGE BRENT) .. other half after death of daughter, ANN SLAUGHTER, to granddaughter, ELEANOR CLIFTON SLAUGHTER .. (same descent) .. I give unto my cousens, WILLIAM BRENT and ROBERT BRENT, of Stafford County .. thirty one slaves (names) .. immediately after my death, my daughter, ANN SLAUGHTER, may and shall elect and choose any thirteen of the above mentioned slaves .. WILLIAM BRENT and ROBERT BRENT shall use profits to maintain ANN SLAUGHTER during the continuance of her marriage with her Husband, THOMAS SLAUGHTER .. (further discussion of use of slaves if ANN SLAUGHTER survives or does not survive her Husband) .. appoint my Cousens, WILLIAM BRENT and ROBERT BRENT of Stafford County, Executors .. this 26th day November 1772.

Presence Mary Peake, Rob. H. Harrison, Elizabeth Clifton
Humphrey Peake

Adds codicil with discussion of the Thirty one slaves .. signed by ELIZABETH CLIFTON and same witnesses. In another codicil .. appoints GEORGE WASHINGTON Esqr. another Trustee and Executor .. and gives unto my cousen, ANN BRENT, a further legacy of Fifteen pounds current money to be paid her annually during the time she shall live unmarried .. 27th day March 1773.

Presence Mary x Sheridan, Elizabeth Clifton
Geo: Brent, Wm. Rumney,
Robert Hanson Harrison

At a court held .. 17th May 1773 .. will presented by ROBERT BRENT .. and admitted to record.

pp. 229-230 Additional Inventory and Appraisement of the Estate of MARY JOHNSTON Decd taken and made September the 26th 1774 .. items valued and totalled, £ 239.18.4½ .. made by appraisers WM. REARDON, W. COURTS,

MARTIN COCKBURN.
At a court held .. June 20th 1775 .. inventory and appraisement returned and ordered to be recorded.

pp. Will of WILLIAM GOSSAM. The Last Will and Testament of WILLIAM
230- GOSSAM being in a weak and very Low state of health .. leave to my
231 beloved wife, GRACE GOSSAM, a childs part of all my personal estate .. after my wife hath taken the part above mentioned that all the rest of my personal estate be Equally divided amongst my sons and daughters which are THOMAS GOSSAM, JESSE GOSSAM, JOHN GOSSAM, ELIZABETH SUDDATH, MARY GOSSAM, JAMES TUTTLE, JOHN BABTIST TUTTLE, WILLIAM TUTTLE, CHARITY BUCHANAN to the care and management of GRACE GOSSAM and THOMAS GOSSAM, Executors .. this 12th day June 1775.

Test William King, William x Gossam
John x Spragg, Joseph Jacobs Senr.

We GRACE GOSSAM and THOMAS GOSSAM, Executors appointed by the last will and testament of WILLIAM GOSSAM Deceased do hereby certify .. that we do refuse to act as Executors .. further it is our desire that administration of the Estate of the Deced (with the will annexed) may be granted to ALESANDER HENDERSON who is the greatest and almost the only creditor .. given this 12th June 1775.

Grace x Gossam
Witness Sampson Turley, Thos. Gossam
James Rattray, Pet. Wagener

At a court held .. June the 19th 1775 .. will presented by ALEXANDER HENDERSON, Gent. .. ordered to be recorded .. ALEXANDER HENDERSON hath a certificate for obtaining letters of administration in due form.

pp. The Inventory of the Estate of Mr. JOHN CLARK Decd taken by BAR-
231- BARY CLARK and JOHN CLARK, Executors .. no value assigned items ..
232 At a court held .. July 17th 1775 .. inventory returned and ordered to be recorded.

pp. We the Subscribers have Inventoryed and appraised all the Estate
232- of WILLIAM BRONAUGH Deceased that was presented to our view .. items
233 valued and totalled, £ 46.4.4 .. made by appraisers ROBERT BOGGESS, GILBERT SIMPSON, WM. BAYLY.

The Sails of the Estate of WILLIAM BRONAUGH .. purchasers include Yelverton Reardon, John Reardon, William Reardon, Mary Ann Bronaugh, John Reardon, Gilbert Simpson, Daniel Ragan, Robert Boggess, Jacob Edwards, William Coloston, Benjamin Cage, Peter Colter, Lenord Atchison, James Luin Gibbs .. cry'd by William Reardon .. amount of sale £ 53.0.10 ..

At a court held .. 21st August 1775 .. inventory and sale of Estate returned and ordered to be recorded.

pp. Fairfax County May 19th 1775. We the Subscribers .. have Inven-
233- toryed and appraised all the Estate of MRS. ELIZABETH CLIFTON, Deceased
235 that was presented to our view in current money .. items valued and totalled, £ 602.14.11 .. made by appraisers THOMAS TRIPLETT, HUMPHREY PEAKE, ABEDNEGO ADAMS.

At a court held .. 18th September 1775 .. inventory and appraisement returned and ordered to be recorded.

p. Will of CHARLES CORNISH. September ye 1st 1775. The last will
235 and testament of CHARLES CORNISH being in a very weak and low state of health .. give to my God son, WILLIAM HOLLYMAN, one cow and calf; to WILLIAM HAZARD the Right and Property of the Plantation I hold on Sandy Run after the decease of my wife, ELIZABETH CORNISH .. I bequeath to my beloved wife, ELIZABETH CORNISH, all other Rights and Properties of my Personal Estate .. likewise appoint her Executrix ..

Test William King,
Benjamin x Suddath, John Eaton

Charles x Cornish

At a court held .. October 16th 1775 .. will presented by ELIZABETH CORNISH .. ordered to be recorded .. certificate granted her for obtaining a probate thereof ..

pp. An Inventory and Appraisement of the Estate of WILLIAM GOSSOM
235- Taken this 11th day September 1775 .. items valued and totalled,
238 £ 66.7.0 .. made by appraisers JOHN HAMPTON, JOHN REID, WILLIAM HANEY.

Sale of the Estate of WILLIAM GOSSOM on 21st September 1775 on credit till the 1st of January 1776 .. purchasers .. Thomas Gossom, George Simpson, George Tillett, Thomas Sangster, Joseph Buchanan, Alexander Henderson .. amounting to £ 81.16.6 ..

At a court held .. 16th October 1775 .. Inventory and appraisement with the sales of the Estate were returned by ALEXANDER HENDERSON, Gent., administrator and ordered to be recorded.

pp. An Inventory of CHARLES CORNISH'S Estate Deceased .. items valued
238- and totalled, £ 137.1.0 .. Fairfax County 26th October 1775 .. We the
239 Subscribers have Inventoryed and appraised the Estate of CHARLES CORNISH Deceased presented to our view by the Executrix .. appraisers THOMAS x WINDSOR, BENJAMIN x SUDARD, JOHN REID.

At a court held .. November 21st 1775 .. Inventory and appraisement returned and ordered to be recorded.

pp. Will of OWEN WILLIAMS. I OWEN WILLIAMS of Parish of Fairfax in
240- Fairfax County being in perfect senses .. give and bequeath to my well
241 beloved son, JEREMIAH WILLIAMS, a tract of land whereon he lives containing 288 acres with three negroes with what stock and furniture he now possesses .. at his decease to heirs of his body lawfully begotten and for want of such heirs to return to ANN JENNINGS and JEMIMA JENKINS to be equally divided between them and then descend to such heirs as they think proper to give it to. I bequeath to my well beloved daughter, JEMIMA JENKINS, two young negroes .. bed and furniture I usually lie on with one half of the Plantation and Tract of land I now live on and at her mother's decease said JEMIMA JENKINS is to possess the whole tract of land and premises. I bequeath to my daughter, ELIZABETH JENNINGS, one cow and calf and one years schooling. I bequeath to my daughter, ANN JENNINGS, five pounds to be made up out of the crop of Tobacco that is inspected .. I leave the use of half the plantation and Houses I now possess with half the plantation I leased to Mr. SAMPSON DARRELL to the use of my well beloved wife, KAZIA WILLIAMS, with the use of two negroes .. at wifes Decease to be equally divided between JEREMIAH WILLIAMS and JEMIMA JENKINS .. remainder of Estate at decease of wife be equally divided between ELIZABETH JENNINGS, ROBERT JENNINGS and ANN JENNINGS, daughter of DANIEL JENNINGS, and JEMIMA JENKINS .. this 21st day April 1769.

Presence Thomas Grafford,
Thos. Trammell

Owen Williams

At a court held .. 19th Febry. 1776 .. will proved .. ordered to be recorded ..

At a court held .. xxth May in year aforesaid, KEZIAH WILLIAMS made oath .. certificate is granted her for obtaining a probate thereof ..

pp. 241-242 Will of WILLIAM LESTER. I WILLIAM LESTER of County and Parish of Fairfax being very sick .. desiring my Brother, THOMAS LESTER, to be sole Executor .. my Estate be equally divided among all my children and to be paid to them as they come to lawfull age. I desire my sons, WILLIAM and VINCENT, may be bound to such Trades as they shall choose .. this 26th day of January 1776.

Presence of James x Maccarty, William Lester
Daniel Jening, William x Seres

At a court held .. xixth day February 1776 .. will presented .. admitted to record .. certificate is granted for obtaining a probate ..

pp. 242-243 Will of HENRY WISHEART. I HENRY WISHEART late of Huntly in County of Loudoun and Colony of Virginia being at this time writing in a very indifferent state of health .. give and bequeath to my youngest daughter, CHARLOTTE WISHEART (meaning the first shall be last and the last shall be first) the sum of Two hundred pounds current money of Virginia .. two negro girls to be delivered when she marries or arrives to age of twenty one; unto my second daughter, JEAN WISHEART, Two hundred pounds current money of Virginia and one young negro fellow which two legacys above mentioned is to be paid in two bonds for Huntly Lands in Loudoun County .. due by MARMADUKE BECKWITH & THOMAS POLLARD his Security both of the county of Fairfax .. (girls) maintained upon Interest thereof and the hire of Negro George who is now hired to DEMSE CARROLL of Loudoun County at Twelve pounds per annum .. bequeath to my eldest daughter, PEGGY WISHEART, the sum of Two hundred pounds current money of Virginia and one negro wench to be delivered to her on day of marriage or when she shall arrive to age of one & twenty .. I expressly stipulate that if any of the above three Sisters should marry clandestinely or without the consent of one of my Executors, as I appoint them my Guardians, she so transgressin her whole fortune shall be given to and equally divided between her other two sisters. I appoint Capt. JOHN DALTON of Alexandria Merchant, Mr. PATRICK COUTS of Richmond Town, James River Merchant, and his Brother, the Revd. MR. WILLIAM COUTTS, Rector of Martins Brandon parish prince george county, Executors as also guardian of my daughters .. this 31st day of January 1776.

Presence of George Simpson, Henry Wisheart
Benjamin Southard, William Simpson

At a court held .. xixth February 1776 .. will presented by JOHN DALTON .. admitted to record .. a certificate is granted him for obtaining a probate thereof ..

pp. 243-244 Will of MERCY CHEW. I MERCY CHEW of the Town of Alexandria in Virginia being sick and weak .. bequeath to my Brother, PHILIP JACKSON, Fifteen pounds; to my loving daughter ANN RUTH GARVEY, now in the Island of St. Kits all my wearing apparel .. also my old negro wench if she can conveniently be sent to her in the meantime that she be hired out and the profits arising be paid my daughter; to my granddaughter, ANN RUTH GARVEY, the daughter of LUCAS and ANN RUTH GARVEY, in the Island of St. Kits, my lot of ground lying on Fairfax and Queen streets in Town of Alexandria (on her arriving at age of Eighteen). My will that my Executors rent out on ground rent forever said part of the said Lot as they may judge best for the benefit of my granddaughter .. to be paid her Father, LUCAS GARVEY .. in case of the death of my granddaughter without heirs I bequeath my said Lot to my grandsons, LUCAS & JOHN GARVEY, to be equally divided betwixt them .. to my son, WILLIAM MANDUIT, Merchant in London and my daughter, ANN RUTH GARVEY, the whole remainder of my Estate .. out of my daughters portion fifty pounds be paid my son in law, LUCAS GARVEY, for mourning. I appoint JOHN DALTON, GEORGE GILPIN and ROBERT HANSON HARRISON Executors .. this 1st November 1775.

Presence Richard Arell, Mercy Chew
Edward Owens, Saml. Arell

At a court held .. xixth day February 1776 .. will proved and admitted to record .. and

At a court held xxth May in the year aforesaid JOHN DALTON and GEORGE GILPIN made oath .. certificate granted them for obtaining a probate thereof ..

pp. 244-245 Will of MARGERY SMITH. I MARGERY SMITH of parish and county of Fairfax being sick and weak in body .. the remainder of my Estate after all of my just debts i give and bequeath unto JEAN CURRAN, MARGRET GOULDY & JOHN YOUNG to be equally divided among them .. excepting one red cow I give to MARGRET GOULDY over and above her part. I give to NANCY LIVISTON my present servant woman one year of her time specified in her Indenture and appoint MARGRET GOULDY and JEAN CURRAN to be Executors .. this 27th day November 1775.

Presence James Connell, Margery x Smith
Roger Chew, John Biggs

At a court held .. xxth February 1776 .. will proved .. ordered to be recorded ..

At a court held .. 18th March in the year afsd, MARGARET GOLDING and JANE CONRAD made oath .. certificate granted them for obtaining a probate thereof ..

p. 245 An appraisement of the Estate of JOHN PRESCOTT deceased .. items valued but not totalled .. made by appraisers THOMAS TRIPLETT, HUMPHREY PEAKE, ABEDNEGO ADAMS, March 17th 1774.

At a court held .. xxth day May 1776 .. inventory returned & ordered to be recorded.

pp. 246-247 November 23d 1775. We the Subscribers .. have Inventoryed and appraised all the Estate of Mr. JOHN BARRY decd in current money .. items valued but not totalled .. made by appraisers THOMAS TRIPLETT, HUMPHREY PEAK, ABEDNEGO ADAMS.

At a court held .. xxth day May 1776 .. inventory returned and ordered to be recorded.

p. 247 1776. The Estate of GEORGE DARRELL deceased. DR. John Muir, Benjamin Hitcheson, John Cannon, John Lowe, Charles Turner, John Sharpe, Francis Summers, William Courts, John Thornton, John Gunnell, James Kirk, George Alexander, James Stuart, Peirce Bayly, Michael Gretter, Richard Arell, Thomas Kirkpatrick, Robert Adam, Anthony Ramsay, John Rhodes, Philip Darrell .. total £ 104.2.18 .. by the Inventory of his

Estate, £ 89.0.6.
At a court held .. xxith May 1776 .. SAMPSON DARRELL admor. of GEORGE DARRELL decd exhibited this account .. is allowed and ordered to be recorded.

p. 248 1774. Dr. The Estate of MARY MOORE deceased with JAMES MOORE administrator .. paid John Atchison his acct, John Rany for making coffin, Richd. Lightfoot for making shoes, John Mays overseers one fifth, Col. George Mason for rent, John Gunnell, paid CLEON MOORE for settling the Estate account, Interest to Marcellus Littlejohn, Wm. Bronaugh, Sarah Littleton (sic), Mary Bucklin and Ann Bucklin daughters to the deceased.
CR. Wm. Bronaugh and John Bates valued 12 hoggs which the admor. could not let remain on the plantation til admor. was granted him since which as the decedent died late in the fall was not done till the spring the court not setting in the Winter, received of John Heaton for debt due estate.
At a court held .. xxth day May 1776 .. JAMES MOORE administrator of MARY MOORE deceased exhibited this account .. is allowed and ordered to be recorded.

pp. 249-250 We have Inventoryed and appraised the slaves and personal estate of PETER WAGENER, Gent. deceased in current money which came to our view .. items valued and totalled, £ 1215.10.0 .. made by appraisers JOHN GIBSON, WM. THOMPSON, WM. BAYLY.
At a court held .. 16th September 1776 .. inventory returned & ordered to be recorded.

p. 251 We the Subscribers .. have inventoried and appraised the slaves of Major PETER WAGENER deceased in Loudoun County and which were presented to our view by SPENCE GRAYSON .. 4 negroes listed .. appraised value, £ 201.0.0 .. given 11th October 1774 .. made by appraisers ANTHONY RUSSELL, JOHN SKILMAN, THOS. PRITCHARD.
At a court held .. 16th September 1776 .. inventory returned and ordered to be recorded.

p. 251 We the Subscribers have inventoried & appraised all the slaves & personal estate of PETER WAGENER Gent. decd in county of Fauquier which was presented to our view .. two negroes listed with an appraised value of £ 135.0.0 .. total valuation £ 199.10.0 .. made by appraisers BEN: HARRISON, WM. CONWAY, W. COURTS ..
At a court held .. 16th September 1776 .. inventory returned and ordered to be recorded.

p. 251 We the Subscribers .. have inventoried all the slaves & personal estate of PETER WAGENER Gent. deceased in Dunmore County which was presented to our view .. 13 negroes listed with appraised value, £ 500.0.0 .. total valuation, £ 649.6.6 .. made by appraisers W. COURTS, BENJA. GAINS, ANTHY. HUGHES.
At a court held .. 16th September 1776 .. inventory returned and ordered to be recorded.

p. 252 We the Subscribers .. inventoried & appraised the Estate of OWEN WILLIAMS deceased .. items valued but not totalled .. made by appraisers WILLIAM GUNNELL SENR., HENRY DARNE, WILLIAM DARNE ..
At a court held .. September 16th 1776 .. inventory returned and ordered to be recorded.

p. 252 Will of WILLIAM PAYNE. I WILLIAM PAYNE OF Parish of Fairfax in county of Fairfax being in perfect sense and memory .. give all my Estate only what I have already given by Deeds of Gifts to my four suns, WM. PAYNE, EDWARD PAYNE, SANFORD PAYNE and JOHN PAYNE, to be equally divided between my wife and all my suns and Daughters if they come to demand their parts within one year after my death, if not the part not demanded to go to my suns, WM. PAYNE and JOHN PAYNE .. my desire my sun, EDWARD PAYNE, have the possession care and education of my sun, JOHN PAYNE, & his Estate until he shall come to age of Eighteen years or Twenty one years as my sun, EDWARD, shall think fit. I appoint my son, EDWARD PAYNE, Executor .. the plantation whereon I now live if my wife chuses to live on it she may not be disturbed and in case she dont chuse to live on the plantation then my son, EDWARD PAYNE, have it .. this 20th day of June 1769 ..

Presence of John Richards Wm. Payne
William Richards

At a court held .. 16th September 1776 .. will presented .. being proved is ordered to be recorded .. certificate granted for obtaining a probate thereof ..

p. 253 We the Subscribers .. have inventoryed and appraised all the Estate of JOHN WARD deceased in current money .. items valued but not totalled .. made by appraisers JOHN SUMMERS the Elder, SIMON PEARSON, JEREMIAH WILLIAMS ..

At a court held .. xxith day October 1776 .. inventory returned & ordered to be recorded.

p. 253 Will of ELIZABETH CORNISH. October 9th 1776. The last will and testament of ELIZABETH CORNISH being in a very weak and low state of Health .. give to my Goddaughter, JEMIMA WINDSOR, my side saddle; give MARY HOLYMON my sorrell horse; give BENJAMIN READ the chest that stands in the Shed; give MARY McKENNY all my wearing cloths .. any remainder I give to my brother's youngest child be it either girl or boy and to KATHARINE HOLYMON and the same to be sold and equally divided betwixt them and also I appoint WILLIAM KING Executor ..

Presence of William x Mills, Elizabeth x Cornish
Jeann x Roe

At a court held .. 21st October 1776 .. will proved and admitted to record .. WILLIAM KING refused .. a certificate is granted ALEXANDER HENDERSON Gent. to obtain letters of administration with the will annexed ..

pp. 253-254 Fairfax County. We the Subscribers have met at the late dwelling house of Mr. WM. TRAMMELLS decd .. appraised an Inventory of the Goods & Chattels which were produced to our view this first day of July 1776 .. items valued and totalled, £ 391.0.6 .. made by appraisers BENJN. MOODY, JOHN HUNTER, JOHN JACKSON.

August 7th 1776. We the Subscribers have met at the request of Mr. Trammell to appraise the remainder of the Goods & Chattels presented to our view .. items valued and totalled, £ 415.4.4 .. made by appraisers JOHN HUNTER, JOHN JACKSON.

At a court held .. xxith day October 1776 .. inventory returned and ordered to be recorded.

pp. 254-255 Loudoun County. We the Subscribers have met at the late dwelling house of Mr. WILLIAM TRAMMELL decd .. have appraised an Inventory of the Goods & Chattels which were presented to our view .. items valued

but not totalled .. made by appraisers ROGER WIGGINTON, SPENCER WIGGINTON, THOMAS FINCH.
At a court held .. xxith day October 1776 .. inventory returned and ordered to be recorded.

p. 255 Will of JOHN WILLIAMS. I JOHN WILLIAMS of Fairfax County being weak in body .. give and bequeath to my loveing wife, SARAH WILLIAMS, one gray Gelding, one bed & furniture and one negro wench and a negro girl .. above legacy at her death to be divided amongst her children as she thinks fit. My will that the rest of my Estate be equally divided amongst my wife and children .. my wife, SARAH WILLIAMS, shall be Executrix .. this first day March 1776 ..
Witness John Keith, John x Williams
Thomas Sinclair, Sampson Darrell
At a court held .. 19th November 1776 .. will presented .. admitted to record .. certificate granted her for obtaining a probate ..

pp. 255-256 We the Subscribers .. did meet and appraise the Estate of JOHN LOCK WILLIAMS decd as was presented to our view .. items valued and totalled, £ 208.4.9, made by appraisers AUGUSTUS DARRELL, JOHN KEITH, JOHN x COMPTON.
At a court held .. 16th December 1776 .. inventory returned & ordered to be recorded.

p. 256 We the Subscribers .. hath viewed and appraised the goods and Chattels of AARON CLARK deceased shewn to us by BENJAMIN RYLEY .. items valued but not totalled .. made by appraisers BARTIN MARTIN, JOHN WARD, GRAFTON KIRKE ..
At a court held .. 16th December 1776 .. inventory returned & ordered to be recorded.

p. 257 Will of THOMAS FORD. August 29th 1774. I THOMAS FORD of Fairfax County being week of body .. give and bequeath to my loving wife, JANE FORD, the use of the plantation whereon I now live and all the land lying between the long branch and the Rattlesnake branch not interrupting of JOSEPH WOODS Lease during her natural life .. also use of two slaves .. after her decease slaves to be sold .. money equally divided among my four daughters, ELIZABETH FORD the widow of WILLIAM KING, ANN FORD the wife of JOHN POSEY, CATY FORD the wife of JOHN SIMPSON, and PRISCILLA FORD the wife of JOSIAH FERGUSON. I give to my beloved son, JOHN FORD, one half of the land I possess at the loer end of the tract whereon I live. The other half I give to my well beloved son, EDWARD FORD, at the upper end of the tract where JAMES MOORE now lives. I give my well beloved daughter, CATY FORD, the wife of JOHN SIMPSON, one feather bed & furniture and one cow & calf; unto my daughter, SARAH FORD, wife of THOMAS JACOBS, five pounds current money; unto my granddaughter, MARY JACOBS, a suit of apparel. I leave my wife, JANE FORD, and my son, EDWARD FORD, Executors ..
Test William x Coe, Thomas Ford
Jane x Coe, William Coe Junr., John Coe
At a court held .. 16th December 1776 .. will presented by EDWARD FORD .. admitted to record .. certificate is granted him for obtaining a probate thereof ..

pp. 257-258 Will of GEORGE HUNTER. I GEORGE HUNTER of parish of Fairfax in county of Fairfax being in perfect health .. give and bequeath to my Hond. Mother, ELIZABETH HUNTER, all the stock & furniture belonging to me in the Estate of my Deceased Father .. to my Brother, JOHN CHAPMAN HUNTER, the tract of land lying in Fairfax County left me by my Father .. provided he pay my sister, AMELIA TERRETT, Fifty pounds current money of Virginia for buying a negro girl .. to my Brother, NATHANIEL CHAPMAN HUNTER, all the negroes I shall be entitled to from my Fathers estate .. on condition he pay my Sister, MARGARET HUNTER, Fifty pounds Virginia currency to dispose of as she pleases for I am sensible she would not choose to be restricted in her purchase. In consideration of the esteem and love I bear my uncle, GEORGE CHAPMAN, I give and bequeath to him Ten Guineas for the purchase of a ring to wear as a mememto of my regard this seventeenth day of May 1766.

Presence of Robert Muir, G. Hunter
Henry Gunnell

At a court held .. 16th December 1776 .. will was proved & ordered to be recorded.

End of Fairfax County Will Book C.

P. WAGENER Cl Cur.

(Note on last page: Examined. O. GUNNELL 1854.)

FAIRFAX COUNTY, VIRGINIA

WILL BOOK D

20 January 1777 - 16 December 1783

pp. 1-2 Will of MARY GOARD. I MARY GOARD of Town of Alexandria in county of Fairfax and State of Virginia being of sound & disposing mind .. bequeath unto my grandson, JOHN DENNIS SCOTT, the house and Lott whereon I now live .. if he should dye before he comes of age then should go to the sons of my Eldest son, JOSEPH JOANES .. desire my son, JOSEPH JOANES, should keep the lott for which he has a deed joyning CHARLES TURNER Deed. Also my son, JOHN SCOTT alies TARBUCK, the lott in the old field for which he has a Deed .. whatever is left after paying my debts I give the same to my grandson, JOHN DENNIS SCOTT .. appoint my Friend, Mr. JOHN CARLYLE & Capt. JOHN WEST JUNR. Executors .. this 10th day November 1776 ..

Presence Wm. Ramsay, Mary x Goard
Mary Shaw, Sarah Simons

At a court held .. xxth day January 1777 .. will presented by JOHN CARLYLE Gent. .. being proved is admitted to record .. certificate is granted him for obtaining a probate thereof ..

p. 2 November 22d 1773. We the Subscribers .. have appraised all the Estate of WILLIAM FRYAR Deceased which was brought to our view .. items valued and totalled, £ 52 (remainder missing) .. made by appraisers

DANIEL KINCHELOE, JAS. WAUGH, SAMUEL TILLETT.
At a court held .. 17th February 1777 .. inventory returned and ordered to be recorded.

p. 3 Will of AUGUSTUS DARRELL. I AUGUSTUS DARRELL of Fairfax County being weak in body .. give to my wife, SARAH DARRELL, what the law will allow her and at her death her part so left shall be Equally divided between WILLIAM DARRELL, PHILIP DARRELL, SAMPSON DARRELL, ELIZABETH DARRELL, CORDELIA DARRELL & ANN DARRELL .. the residue of my Estate shall be equally divided amongst my above mentioned Brothers and Sisters .. my will my father, SAMPSON DARRELL, should be my Executor .. this 16th day of January 1777.
Witness Humphrey Peake, Augustus Darrell
Francis Adams, Alexander Cleveland
At a court held .. 17th February 1777 .. will presented by SAMPSON DARRELL .. proved is admitted to record .. certificate is granted him for obtaining a probate thereof ..

pp. 4-6 Will of JOHN WEST JUNR. I JOHN WEST, son of HUGH WEST late of County of Fairfax deceased, being at this time of sound mind .. give and bequeath to my Eldest son, THOMAS WEST, my track of land whereon my Mother lives containing 627 acres and also one half of the land purchased of TERRETT .. to my son, JOHN WEST, the other half part of the land purchased of TERRETT & also all the track of land purchased of BURR HARRISON together with the Pocoson adjacent to him .. unto my son, HUGH WEST, my track of land joyning to JOHN SUMMERS containing about 400 acres. I give all my Ohio lands to be Equally divided among all my Sons & Daughters excepting that I desire my son, HUGH, have one thousand acres more than any of the rest of my children .. to my Brother, GEORGE WEST, a small track of land taken up by my Father containing about 27 acres joining his other track purchased of NOLAND .. and whereas Collo. THOMAS COLVILL lately deceased after several bequeaths appoints the residue of his estate (if any) to be divided into four equal parts & bequeaths to each one fourth part to one Stott, Wills, Richardson & Smith provided they prove their relationship to him within five years after his death .. if they fail to do so said residue to descend to my children as I see fit .. if they fail what part thereof lawfully descending to my children be equally divided among all my children .. desire my Executors to divide the Track of land purchased of TERRETT between my sons, THOMAS & JOHN .. remainder not bequeathed to be equally divided among my children, THOMAS, JOHN, CATHARINE, FRANCES, SARAH & HUGH, the boys to be intitled to their proportions at age of Twenty one years, the girls .. on day of marriage or when they arrive to age Twenty one years ..appoint GEORGE WEST and the REVEREND WILLIAM WEST (my Brothers) together with my son, THOMAS, Executors .. this 26th day April 1775.
Presence Sarah x Lewis, John West Junr.
S. West, Wm. Triplett
At a court held .. 18th February 1777 .. will proved by the oaths of SIBYL WEST and WILLIAM TRIPLETT .. ordered to be recorded ..
At a court held .. 21st April in the year aforesaid, GEORGE WEST and WILLIAM WEST, Cl, having performed what the Law requires, certificate is granted them for obtaining a probate thereof ..

p. 6 An Inventory of Goods & Chattles and Credits of WILLIAM BRADLEY late of Fairfax County Deceased .. items valued and totalled, £ 25.10.6 .. given 15th day September 1775 by appraisers THOMAS GUNNELL, HENRY BURNAM, JOHN SHIPPARD.

At a court held .. 17th March 1777 .. inventory returned and ordered to be recorded.

pp. 7-8 An appraisement Inventory of the Personal Estate late property of THOMAS FORD Deceased of Fairfax County appraised by JOHN TILLETT, MOSES SIMPSON & FRANCIS COFFEER .. sworn for that purpose .. items valued but not totalled ..

At a court held .. 17th March 1777 .. inventory returned and ordered to be recorded.

pp. 8-9 Will of MARY HAWKINS. I MARY HAWKINS of Colony of Virginia in Fairfax County being in very low state of health .. give and bequeath to my son, JAMES HAWKINS, one new desk that he now makes use of; to my son, JOHN HAWKINS, one new Desk. It is my will and desire that my Books be put in proper hands to collect the debts that is due and as the money is collected from time to time to be equally divided amongst all my children to support them & pay for their schooling and after my sons, THOMAS & RANDOLPH HAWKINS, have got their Education it is my desire that they be put to some trade or business. I give to my Daughter, ELENOR HAWKINS, one negro woman and her child .. all my wearing apperial .. parcel of new goods in the house for cloathes for her .. residue to be sold .. and after debts paid equally divided amongst all my children .. desire my sons, JOHN & JAMES HAWKINS, be Executors and Capt. PHILIP ALEXANDER & FRANCIS H. MARBURY Trustees & Managers of the Estate for my children .. this 4th day of May 1777.

Witness Adam Lynn, Mary x Hawkins
Peter Wise, Francis H. Marbury

At a court held .. 16th June 1777 .. will presented by JAMES HAWKINS .. admitted to record .. certificate granted him for obtaining a probate thereof ..

pp. 9-11 Will of JAMES CONNILL. I JAMES CONNILL being at this time in my sound Judgment but weak in body desire that the following Division be made of my Estate .. debts be paid .. house and Tenements be given to JOHN SUTTON, Watch Maker in Carlyle .. he making following payments. To pay MARY CHAMBERS, wife of STEPHEN CHAMBERS of Flimby in Cumberland County one hundred pounds current money of Virginia or Eighty pounds Sterling money of Great Britain and in the second place that my shop and hoshold Furniture & Books be sold at publick sale not excepting my dear wife's wearing apperil .. give a certain WILLIAM BLYSTON, son of a certain CATHERINE BLYSTON, the sum of Forty pounds Virginia money to be laid out on the Education of said WILLIAM BLYSTON .. if he dies money not laid out with Fifty pounds additional be given to NANCY, the daughter of a certain MARGARET SCREVINER now in my service .. my Executors deliver to ROBERT & THOMAS FREDERICK now my apprentice who I discharge from any further service, the following tools, Two hand saws, one pannel saw, two long plains, two Jack plains, three smoothing plains, six hand saw files, six mortice chizels, one inch Oger, one half inch oger, one half inch bead plain, one five eight bead plain, one sliding Rule .. my Friend, Mr. WILLIAM RAMSAY, Mr. JAMES KIRK & ROBERT ADAM or any two of them be my Executors .. this 17th day May

1777 ..
Presence Thomas Crafts, James Connill
Thomas Kirkpatrick, James Adam,
William Brown

At a court held .. 16th June 1777 .. will presented by WILLIAM RAMSAY & ROBERT ADAM .. admitted to record .. certificate is granted them for obtaining a probate thereof ..

pp. 11-14 An appraisement of the personal estate of WILLIAM SHAW Deceased taken by us the Subscribers appointed by the Court .. mentions white servant boy, PETER SWANEY, PETER HOLMS, RICHARD STEUART, HENRY HALL .. parcel of Sailers bed cloathes .. made by appraisers JAMES CONNILL, ROBERT McCREA, JAMES HENDRICKS.

At a court held .. 21st July 1777 .. inventory returned and ordered to be recorded.

After Advertisements no Bidders appearing for the Estate of WILLIAM SHAW Deceased, the servants were sold at private sale .. John Peter Holm, Richard Steuart, Henry Hall to MATHEW CAMPBELL; Mr. KIRKPATRICK, STACKHOUSE History of the Bible .. also books to ANDREW WALES, CHARLES TURNER (Edinburgh News Papers), JOHN BROOKS .. other items to William Brown, Mrs. SHAW, Thomas Moxley, Charles Broadwater Junr., John Orr, Alexander Chisholm, John Graham (suit of Buff & blue Regementals), John Harper, John Lomax, Richard Arell, JOHN SHAW .. sale value recorded but not totalled ..

At a court held .. 21st July 1777 .. Sale returned and ordered to be recorded.

pp. 14-15 Will of THOMAS TAYLOR. I THOMAS TAYLOR of Fairfax County being weak and sick in body .. give and bequeath to my son, THOMAS TAYLOR, my part of a track of land lying in Prince George County Maryland Government known by the name of little grove .. (other items) .. to my son, RICHARD TAYLOR, one Fether Bed and one yeo and Lam .. give to my beloved wife the hole of my Estate during her natural life and then to be Equally divided between my Daughters, SARAH TAYLOR, CLOEANN TAYLOR, EUNIS TAYLOR, MILORD TAYLOR, ARRYBECKEY TAYLOR and my Daughter, DRUSILLA TAYLOR, and my sons, THOMAS TAYLOR and JOHN TAYLOR and BAZEL TAYLOR .. my plantation I now live on to my son, THOMAS TAYLOR .. to my son, BENJAMIN BASSICK TAYLOR one shilling sterling .. to my daughter, BARBARA STUART, one shilling sterling .. to my daughter, MARY ANN CLUB, one shilling sterling .. leave my son, THOMAS TAYLOR, Executor .. 1777 June 11th.

Witness Robert Boggess Thomas Taylor
Rodham Rogers

At a court held .. 21st July 1777 .. will presented by THOMAS TAYLOR .. admitted to record .. certificate granted to him for obtaining a probate thereof ..

pp. 15-16 We the Subscribers have valued & appraised all the Estate of JOHN POTTOTH Deceased .. items valued but not totalled .. made by appraisers JOHN BARRY, JAMES BROWN, DANIEL STONE ..

At a court held .. 21st July 1777 .. inventory returned and ordered to be recorded.

pp. 17-20 Will of JOHN DALTON. I JOHN DALTON of the Town of Alexandria do make this my last will and testament .. give and bequeath to my daughter, JENNY DALTON, that part of my lots whereon I live beginning at the corner of my new brick house .. with the lines of the Lotts on Cameron street down to Potowmack River and in part on Fairfax street so as to include the said Brickhouse & three feet more towards my dwelling house .. my will is that said house be finished out of my Estate .. to my daughter, CATHERINE, the remaining part of my said lotts .. corner of the lot which is ten feet beyond the House wherein JOHN PAGE now lives, the ten feet is left vacant in order that ALEXANDER HENDERSON or those claiming under him may lay off an equal proportion of his Lots that a line may be extended down between said Lots to Potowmack River .. as Mr. THOMAS SHAW has bequeathed to my daughter, JENNY, his lands at Cameron, I bequeath to my daughter, CATHARINE, my plantation (meaning) the lands bought of the heirs of WILLIAM HARRISON as well as that bought of CUTHBERT HARRISON containing about 600 acres .. as Mr. THOMAS SHAW holds a Track of land that he bought of THOMAS HARRISON of about 300 acres which of my said daughters he gives the said track to as I hold a moiety of 94 acres taken up and patented in Mr. JOHN CARLYLE'S name & mine which said moiety joins Mr. SHAWS land, I give the said moiety to that daughter the said SHAW gives the adjoining land. To my daughter, CATHARINE, a track of land whereon JOHN BRIDGES lives containing about 200 acres. A track of land bought of JOHN ALLAN with a vacancy annexed on Goose Creek on which RICHARD WHEELER & others live, the deeds for which are in Mr. CARLYLE'S name, also the remainder of the Bloomery Lands the deeds of which are in the hands of Mr. JOHN CARLYLE, also a Lot on Royal & Cameron streets on which is a Brick house formerly the property of CHARLES and ANN MASON but now the property of the Testator & Col. JOHN CARLYLE jointly, also a tract of land on Capepchon bought of WILLIAM CARLYLE, it is my desire they be sold as well as any Lands deeded in our joint names in the back counties, a track bought of ENOCH LEONARD and sold to JACOB HAYZILL a part of which purchase money is paid tho the Deeds are not perfected my will the deeds be perfected .. two lots in Town of Alexandria now in occupation of ROGER CHEW & a baker (Heninger) .. I give unto ANN LONGDEN the use of my moiety .. after her death to be equally divided between her two children, ANN and ROBERT .. also to ANN LONGDEN a feather bed she now uses .. Fifty pounds .. also One hundred pounds the Interest to be paid her annually and also Five pounds annually until her said children come of age .. and if they are living then the said One hundred pounds to be equally divided between them .. I give unto RICHARD MORTON GERRARD Twenty pounds .. JENNY and CATHARINE, granddaughters of THOMAS SHAW .. appoint THOMAS SHAW, JOHN CARLYLE, WILLIAM RAMSAY, WILLIAM HERBERT and DENNIS RAMSAY Executors .. this 9th day of March 1777 ..

Presence Jas. Muir, John Dalton
John Shaw, Roger Chew

At a court held .. 21st July 1777 .. will presented by JOHN CARLYLE, WM. RAMSAY and DENNIS RAMSAY .. admitted to record .. certificate is granted them for obtaining a probate thereof ..

pp. 21-22 We the Subscribers do appraise and Inventory all the Estate of WILLIAM LESTER deceased .. items valued but not totalled .. made by appraisers HENRY GUNNELL, THOMAS GUNNELL, THOMAS LEWIS ..

At a court held .. 21st July 1777 .. Inventory returned and ordered to be recorded.

pp. 22-25 Alexandria 30th June 1777. Inventory of Estate of MARY HAWKINS Deced which was presented to our view & appraised by us .. items valued and totalled, £ 488.15.3 .. made by appraisers JOSH. WATSON, JOHN MUIR, PETER WISE.

At a court held .. 18th August 1777 .. inventory returned and ordered to be recorded.

pp. 25-33 Will of JOHN WEST. I JOHN WEST of parish of Fairfax in county of Fairfax being of sound and disposing mind .. my body to be interred by or near the body of my first wife if I may die at or be convenincy brought to the Place. Whereas I have formerly given to my son in law, DANIEL TALBUT, who married my first daughter, ANN, about 376 acres where he now lives during his natural life the remainder to my grandson, JOHN TALBUT, and in case of JOHN'S death without issue to my granddaughter, MONICA TALBUT .. in case her death without issue to my grandaughter, ELIZABETH TALBUT .. whereas my grandson, JOHN TALBUT, died without issue and the land will descend unto my granddaughter, MONICA TALBUT, after the death of her Father, and my granddaughter, ELIZABETH TALBUT, in all likelyhood will never receive any benefit from said land therefore I give (her) Sixty pounds current money of Virginia to be laid out in the purchase of as young and likely Female negro slave as the sd sum will purchase. Whereas I have already given to my son in law, JOHN ASHTON, and HANNAH, his wife, one young negro woman and Two hundred and Fifty pounds current money .. and whereas I have already given to my son in law, RICHARD CONWAY & MARY, his wife, a young negro woman & Two hundred and fifty pounds current money .. (as much as he intends for HANNAH and MARY) .. bequeath unto my daughter, ANN WEST, one young negro woman, also Two hundred and fifty pounds being the sum due me from Mr. ALEXANDER HENDERSON upon his Penal bill to be paid her upon her day of Marriage provided she marries with consent of her Mother and at least two of my Executors .. also give my Daughter, Ann, Twelve pounds Ten shillings annually to be paid upon the 21st day of June .. if Ann dies before she marries (bequest) to be equally divided between daughters HANNAH ASHTON & MARY CONWAY .. unto my son, ROGER WEST, my dwelling plantation containing 205 acres of land also 295 acres part sunken and part high land which is separate from my dwelling plantation by one corner of 500 acres of land that is now in the possession of Mr. DAVID BOYD (late Capt. WOODBRIDGES land) .. also eleven slaves .. in default of heirs (Roger's bequest) to MARY CONWAY .. also to my son, ROGER WEST, my old Quarter and the land whereon BENJA. BOYLSTON is now overseer containing 450 acres .. and ten slaves .. in default of heirs to HANNAH ASHTON .. to my son, ROGER WEST, my new Quarter of 458 acres of land lying upon the mane road & where CONNER MAGUIRE now teaches school .. also ten slaves .. in default of heirs to my daughter ANN WEST .. if it should happen to descend to my daughter, ANN WEST, by death of her Brother, ROGER .. if she departs this life without issue .. to be equally divided between daughters HANNAH ASHTON & MARY CONWAY .. unto my son, ROGER WEST, my three fishing seins, my Moses boat and Skew and earnestly recommend to my Executors to keep in good repair .. to carry on fishing business as I will know it will be of great Advantage to my son Roger's Estate .. to my son .. one gold ring that was left to him by his sister, ELIZABETH WEST .. I give unto my wife, MARGARET WEST, the care management & Tuition of my daughter, ANN WEST .. if my wife dies .. to the care of my daughters, HANNAH ASHTON & MARY CONWAY .. I give and devise the whole and sole guardianship management care and Tuition of my son, ROGER WEST, and his estate during his Infancy .. unto my good friend, GEORGE WASHINGTON Esqr. .. if he cannot or will not undertake .. secondly to my son in law, RICHARD CONWAY .. if he cannot or will not .. thirdly to my son in law, JOHN ASHTON .. if my son shews any inclination to study divinity, Phisick or Law that he will give him the opportunity first Divinity, secondly Phisick and thirdly Law. I appoint my good friend, GEORGE WASHINGTON Esqr., my three sons in law, DANIEL TALBUT, JOHN ASHTON & RICHARD CONWAY, Executors .. this 27th day of March 1776

John West

Presence Daniel McCarty, Pet: Wagener,
Lund Washington, John Muir

At a court held .. 18th August 1777 .. will proved .. ordered to be recorded.

pp. 34-36 Estate of DANIEL FRENCH, decd .. To GEORGE MASON, acting Executor and Guardian to his daughter, ELIZABETH .. (1774) paid ROBERT ADAM for Brad nails for new church; ZACHARIAH BOND, JAS. LEE for 11½ days work making two fram'd Horseblocks & six benches at the new church at Pohick; to ROBERT BOGGESS for sawing planks for benches & boarding Zacha. Bond& James Lee while they were making horseblocks & benches for the church; PETER WAGENER Clerk of Fairfax County a copy of the decd will & recording the Estate account; (1776) JOHN MILLS for sundry nails, JAS. LEE for horseblocks at Pohick Church omitted in 1774; (1777) to GOING LAMPHIER for measuring valuing the extra work at the Church and attending the Vestry to prove it; (1775) CR. By BENJAMIN DULANY Esqr., ANDREW STEUART on DAVID HERVEY & CO. Mercht. in London ..

At a court held .. 18th August 1777 .. GEORGE MASON .. exhibited this account.. is allowed and ordered to be recorded.

pp. 36-38 Will of SHAPLEIGH NEAL. The Eighth day of June 1777. I SHAPLEIGH NEAL of county of Fairfax being very sick .. give and bequeath to my beloved wife, MARY NEAL, Eight negroes .. to be at her disposal .. one negro .. after wife's death to be divided between Brother, DANIEL NEAL and RICHARD NEAL and my sister, JEMIMA GUNNELL .. the fourth part to be divided between Mr. WISHARTS Daughters, MARGARET WISHART, JEAN WISHEART, CHARLOTTE WISHART .. ordain my beloved wife, MARY NEAL, & ROBERT BOGGESS, my Executors .. I give my wearing apparell to RICHARD NEAL'S sons, RICHD. & GEORGE ..

Presence Robert Boggess, Shapleigh Neal
The mark of Isaac Gates

At a court held .. 18th August 1777 .. will presented by MARY NEAL .. admitted to record .. certificate is granted her for obtaining a probate thereof ..

pp. 38-39 Will of THOMAS SHAW. I THOMAS SHAW of county of Fairfax being weak in body .. give and bequeath unto JENNY DALTON, my granddaughter, all my Track of land which I bought of the Exrs. of Capt. JOHN MINOR as well as the Track of land which I bought of JOHN MINOR commonly known by the name of Cameron which said track with the appurtenances I give unto my said granddaughter .. for want of heirs it returns to JOHN BRIDGES & BAYNHAM SHAW. I give that track of land near the Falls Church which I bought in conjunction with Colo. JOHN CARLYLE of Colo. THOMAS HARRISON unto my granddaughter, CATHERINE DALTON .. for want of heirs to JOHN BRIDGES & BAYNHAM SHAW. I give unto my said granddaughters equally to be divided my personal Estate (only a legacy or two) .. for want of heirs to JOHN BRIDGES & BAYNHAM SHAW. I give to JEMIMA MINOR the sum of Fifteen pounds current money. I appoint GEORGE MINOR, RICHARD SANFORD SENR. and JENNY DALTON to be my Exrs. .. this 29th day of May 1777.

Presence of John Moss, Thomas x Shaw
Robert Muir, Geo. Minor

At a court held .. 18th August 1777 .. will presented by GEORGE MINOR .. admitted to record .. certificate is granted him for obtaining a probate thereof ..

pp. 39-40 Will of PAUL TURLEY. I PAUL TURLEY of Truro Parish in county of Fairfax being of sound mind and memory .. give the whole of my Estate to my Mother, SARAH TURLEY, during her life and after her death .. it shall be equally divided between my Sisters, MARY TURLEY and ELIZABETH TURLEY .. do hereby appoint THOMAS POLLARD Gent. Executor .. this 27th day of June 1777.

Presence of Arthur Edwards, Paul Turley
Alexr. Henderson

At a court held .. 15th Decr. 1777 .. will presented by THOMAS POLLARD .. admitted to record .. certificate granted him for obtaining a probate thereof ..

pp. 40-42 Will of SAMPSON DARRELL. I SAMPSON DARRELL of county of Fairfax & State of Virginia being in perfect senses & memory .. give unto my beloved wife, MARY DARRELL, during her natural life the Plantation whereon I now dwell .. supposed to be 400 acres .. also sundry negroes (names 6) .. give to my son, WILLIAM DARRELL, three negroes .. allso one Feather bed & furniture (cattle and bay mare & colt) .. give to my son at Mother's death all estate given to her .. unto my son, SAMPSON DARRELL, one moiety of a Track of land call'd my Chestnut Land being in Fairfax County near the Letel falls of Potomack, also three negroes .. give unto my son, PHILIP, one moiety of the above track of land .. also three negroes .. unto my daughter, ELIZABETH DARRELL, a small Track of land .. being in Fairfax County within one mile of the Plantation whereon I now dwell also three negroes .. unto my daughter, CORDELIA, three negroes .. unto my daughter, ANN BROOKS, three negroes .. my desire that my son, WILLIAM DARRELL, be my Executor with his Mother, MARY .. this 19th day of October 1777.

Presence Alexander Cleveland, Sampson Darrell
John Harper Senr., Mary x Pinkerman

At a court held .. 15th December 1777 .. will presented by WILLIAM DARRELL & MARY DARRELL .. admitted to record .. certificate is granted them for obtaining a probate thereof ..

p. 43 We the Subscribers have Inventoryed and appraised all the Estate of THOMAS TAYLOR deceased that was presented to our view .. items valued and totalled, £ 372.13.3 .. made by appraisers SOLIAS CLORE, EDWARD x SHELTON, ABEL MARKFIELD.

At a court held .. 19th Jany. 1778 .. inventory returned and ordered to be recorded.

pp. 44-45 DR. Estate of MARGERY SMITH. Payments made to John Smith, Roger Chew, John Williams, Mary Rhodes, John Biggs, Josiah Watson, Joel Cooper, Doctr. Benj. Chapen, William Hunter, Wm. Allison cryer at sale, to Doctr. Wm. Rumney; cash returned to John Muir it being borrowed of him to pay John Biggs & Mr. Wm. Hunter; paid Margaret Golding her third part; Jean Curran her third part; John Young his third part (each received £ 28.3.9) .. Contra. Mr. Walter Bean, Mr. William Herbert, Mr. Nathan Campbell ..

At a court held .. 17th March 1778 .. JOHN MUIR on behalf of MARGARET GOLDING and JEAN CURRAN, Exrs. of MARGERY SMITH, exhibited this account .. is allowed and ordered to be recorded.

pp. 45-46 An inventory & appraisement of goods and affects of Estate of THOMAS BROWNLEY late of Alexandria deceased appraised the 26th day of March 1778 .. includes silver watch and 1 Diamond Glass cutter .. items valued and totalled, £ 49.12.0 .. made by appraisers JOHN GRAHAM, JAMES PARSONS, PETER WISE.

At a court held .. 21st April 1778 .. inventory returned and ordered to be recorded.

pp. 46-47 Alexandria October 4th 1777. An appraisement and Inventory of the goods and effects of the Estate of the late CONSTANTINE DOROTHY deceased taken by PETER WISE, JOHN SHAW and ROGER CHEW. Items valued and totalled, £ 61.1.6 .. includes one great coat, one uniform coat, 2 stript Jackets, one nankeen jacket & pr breeches, 1 pr. Trousers, 2 pr leather breeches, 1 shirt, 2 checked shirts, 1 velvet jacket & breeches, 5 pr stockings, 2 pr shoes, 1 pr buckles, 2 Pocket books, 1 pr Knee buckles, 1 case razors and hone, 1 pr spectacles, 1 linnen jacket and 2 pr breeches, 1 Frock and a wallet, 1 Knap Sack with sundry trifles ..

At a court held .. 21st April 1778 .. inventory returned and ordered to be recorded.

pp. 47-49 Will of ANDREW STEUART. I ANDREW STEUART of Town of Alexandria in county of Fairfax & Colony of Virginia Merchant being in perfect senses and a sound and disposing mind .. give to my Friend, Mr. WILLIAM HERBERT of Town of Alexandria the sum of Five hundred pounds sterling money of Great Britain. I give unto CHARLES McINTIRE and JEAN, his wife, of donegale .. the annual sum of Five pounds sterling. If MARY ANN McINTIRE, daughter of said CHARLES and JEAN McINTIRE, his wife of Donegale in Kingdom of Ireland, shall survive them, the said CHARLES and JEAN, I give unto MARY ANN the sum of Five pounds sterling to be paid her annually .. I give to the children of my Brother, CHARLES STEUART Esquire, of Horn Head in Ireland .. to be equally divided between them as Tenants in Common except his Eldest son who is not to be included in or to claim any thing under this Devise .. all the residue of my Estate .. I give unto ANDREW McINTIRE my waring apparell. I appoint CHARLES STEUART Esqr., JOHN MAXWELL NISBET of City of Philadelphia, DAVID STEUART of Baltimore Town in Maryland and WILLIAM HERBERT of Alexandria Executors .. this 18th day of June 1775.

Presence John Fitzgerald, David Jackson, Val. Peers, Rob. H. Harrison

Andrew Steuart

April 19th 1778. VALENTINE PEERS made oath he saw Testator sign the above instrument of writing as his last will and testament and that he was of sound mind.

Wm. Ramsay, JP

At a court held .. 21st April 1778 .. will presented by WILLIAM HERBERT .. admitted to record .. certificate granted him for obtaining a probate thereof ..

pp. 49-50 1777. DR. Estate of WM. TRAMMELL Decd to SAMPSON TRAMMELL .. payments to Edward Ramsay, Doctor William Brown, John Harl, John Benson. Cr. Thomas Lindsay.

At a court held .. 21st April 1778 .. SAMPSON TRAMMELL administrator of the Estate of WILLIAM TRAMMELL deceased exhibited this account .. is allowed and ordered to be recorded.

pp. 50-55 Fairfax County. We the Subscribers having been first sworn before Colo. GEORGE GILPIN have appraised the Esta. of Colo. JOHN WEST deceased and also set apart and alloted to ROGER WEST so much of said Esta. as is devised to sd ROGER by the sd Will of sd Decd .. items valued and totalled, £ 3678.2.8, which includes 29 negroes with an appraised value of £ 3315.0.0 allotted to ROGER WEST agreeable to the Will of the late Colo. JOHN WEST deceased .. made by appraisers JOHN MUIR, ROBERT McCREA, RICHD. SANFORD, HUMPHREY PEAKE.

Appraisement of the residue of Colo. JOHN WEST'S Estate .. items valued and totalled, £ 1256.14.9, made by same appraisers ..

At a court held .. 21st April 1778 .. inventory returned and ordered to be recorded.

pp. 55-56 We the Subscribers being first sworn before Mr. RICHARD CHICHESTER Gent. have appraised the Estate of RAMOND BURNHAM Deceased in current money & made a true Inventory of the same .. items valued and totalled, £ 23.7.0 .. made the 8th day of January 1778 by appraisers ELIJA. WILLIAMS, DRUMMOND WHEELER, THOS. PALMER ..

At a court held .. 21st April 1778 .. inventory returned and ordered to be recorded.

pp. 56-57 March 14th 1778. An Inventory of the Estate of ANTONY HARRISS Deceased .. items valued and totalled, £ 28.9.6 .. made by appraisers THOMAS GUNNELL, HENRY BURNAM, JOHN SHIPPARD.

At a court held .. 18th May 1778 .. inventory returned and ordered to be recorded.

pp. 57-59 We the Subscribers have appraised all the Estate of HENRY WISHEART deceased that has been presented to our view .. "negroes specifically bequeath'd Cloe & given to Peggy .. £ 70" .. made by appraisers SAMPSON TURLEY, JOHN TILLETT, GEORGE SIMPSON.

At a court held .. 18th May 1778 .. inventory returned and ordered to be recorded.

pp. 59-60 Sales made of Estate of HENRY WISHEART deceased April 1st and 2nd 1776 .. JEAN WISHEART 1 Trunk, 1 Feather bed and Furniture, 1 silver broach; Danl. Atkins, George Simpson, Gilbert Roland, Thomas Songster, Shapleigh Neal, Specticals etc. by Edwd. Washington; Simon Shaver, Francis Coffer, Sampson Turley, Jerrard Barnett, Anthony Rains, John Tillett, Benja. Suddoth, John Martaine,MARGARET WISHEART .. gold ring, side saddle, spinning wheel, cash on hand and purse valued at £ 1.5.0 .. by JOHN DALTON .. total of sale, £ 102.14.7 ..

At a court held .. 18th May 1778 .. Acct of Sales returned and ordered to be recorded.

p. 61 A list of Bonds due Estate of HENRY WISHEART deceased (names that are not already in account of sales previous entry) .. Marmaduke Beckwith, James Waugh, Tyler Waugh, Joseph Brown .. submitted 18th March 1778 by WILLIAM SIMPSON, MOSES SIMPSON. Test. W. ELLZEY. Names THOMAS SHAW, THOMASON ELLZEY as paying notes ..

At a court held .. 18th May 1778 .. List & Receipt returned and ordered to be recorded.

pp. 62-63 HENRY WISHEART Estate to JOHN DALTON Exr. Deceased. DR. Cash for shoes for PEGGY & JENNY, Shapleigh Neal, cash paid Rachel Savage; George Duncan shoes; William Payne sheriffs fees; lists bonds from sale purchases by legatees; John Orr. CR. Received of Sampson Turley, from Thomas Songster, John Martain .. given 21st day of April 1778 by WILLIAM SIMPSON, MOSES SIMPSON. Test. W. ELLZEY.

At a court held .. 18th May 1778 .. Account against Estate of HENRY WISHEART deceased was presented in court by JOHN CARLYLE Gent. .. and ordered to be recorded.

pp. 64-65 Estate of MARY HAWKINS deceased To FRANCIS MARBERRY Trustee for Estate .. cash paid Thomas McPherson, John Lomax, Thomas Warters, Robert Anderson, Mr. Goosling, Thomas Kirkpatrick, Roger Chew, Samuel Hanson, Walter Madox, Michael Gretter, Philip Jackson, Phil. Webster, Robert Adam, Willm. Bushby, Jacob Sunday, Thomas Clagett, Hugh Lyon, Walter Henson, Peter Wise, John Harper, Robt. Hooe. CR. Recd. of Doctor Alexander, Wm. Herbert, Benjn. Dulany, Geo. Muir, Bennett Brown, Paul Parker ..

At a court held .. 22nd September 1778 .. FRANCIS MARBURY Trustee of the Estate of MARY HAWKINS deceased exhibited this account .. is allowed and ordered to be recorded.

pp. 65-66 Will of THOMAS MOSS. I THOMAS MOSS of the county of Fairfax being very sick, weake & in a low state of health & infirm of body .. give ANN GOATLY one Feather bed & furniture, one cow & calf, Two Ews & lambs, one Sow and Piggs, one Pewter dish & 2 basons, give JOHN GOATLY twenty pounds cash .. unto my beloved wife, SARAH MOSS, all my whole Estate not yet mentioned .. at her death bequeath one half of the Estate left her to whom she may think proper .. other half equally divided between JOHN MOSS, ROBERT MOSS, WILLIAM MOSS and THOMAS MOSS .. appoint my beloved wife, SARAH MOSS, & EDWD. DULING my Executors .. this 28th day of January 1778.

Presence Drummond Wheeler, Elija. Williams, Bran. ONeale

Will signed only with a T

At a court held .. 19th May 1778 .. will presented by EDWARD DULIN .. admitted to record .. certificate granted him for obtaining a probate thereof ..

pp. 67-68 Will of SARAH MOSS. I SARAH MOSS of Fairfax County being of perfect mind & memory .. lend to my loving Sister, MARIAN BEATCH .. after her death for her daughter, FRANCES BEATCH .. to my loving Sister, LYDDA HALBERT .. after her decease for her daughter, LIBBY DOVE .. residue to be equally divided between my loving Brothers, WM. DULIN, EDWD. DULIN and JOHN DULIN and my loving Sisters, MARYAN BEATCH, LYDDA HALBERT, ANN SMITH and ANN GOATLY .. appoint my Brothers, EDWD. DULIN and JOHN DULIN, Executors .. this 20th day of Feby 1778.

Presence Sim. Summers, Drummond Wheeler, Frances x Hall

Sarah x Moss

At a court held .. 19th May 1778 .. will presented by EDWARD DULIN .. admitted to record .. certificate is granted him for obtaining a probate thereof ..

p. Estate of WILLIAM LESTER Deceased in acct with THOMAS LESTER Execu-
68 tor .. paying Mr. John Muir, Peter Gollatt, George Killgore, Elizabeth
Simmons .. submitted by THOMAS LESTER August 17th 1778.
At a court held .. 18th August 1778 .. THOMAS LESTER Exor. of WILLIAM LESTER deceased exhibited this account .. is allowed and ordered to be recorded.

pp. An Inventory of the Estate of THOMAS MOSS deceased .. items valued
69- but not totalled .. appraisal of all the Estate of THOMAS MOSS and
72 SARAH his wife that was brought to our view June 18th 1778 .. appraisers CHAS. BROADWATER, JOHN WREN, DRUMMOND WHEELER.
At a court held .. 18th August 1778 .. inventory returned and ordered to be recorded.

p. Account of Sales of Goods contained in the Inventory of the Es-
72 tate of MERCY CHEW deceased .. items valued and totalled, £ 526.3.9
.. made by GEORGE GILPIN Executor ..
At a court held .. 17th August 1778 .. account of sales returned and ordered to be recorded.

pp. Inventory and appraisement of sundry goods and chattles belonging
73- to the Estate of MERCY CHEW deceased .. items valued and totalled,
74 £ 581.15.9 .. included 17 Half Joes, 1 English Guinea, 30¼ Silver
Dollars, 12 paper dollars Maryland curry. .. appraisal made by WM. RAMSAY, JOHN MUIR, WM. HARTSHORNE .. Alexandria 6th May 1778.
At a court held .. 17th August 1778 .. inventory returned and ordered to be recorded.

pp. We the Subscribers being appointed appraisers to appraise the Es-
74- tate of DANL. MILLS BALLANGER deceased .. hath proceeded .. items
75 valued and totalled, £ 42.3.6 .. made by appraisers WM. PAYNE, DANIEL
MILLS, THOMAS x BARKER.
At a court held .. 17th August 1778 .. inventory returned and ordered to be recorded.

pp. We the Subscribers have valued and appraised the Estate of THOMAS
75- SHAW deceased .. items valued and totalled, £ 2148.9.0 .. given the
78 12th day of June 1778 by appraisers GEORGE GILPIN, WM. ADAMS, CHARLES
LITTLE ..
At a court held .. 15th June 1778 .. inventory returned and ordered to be recorded.

p. We the Subscribers have divided the Estate of JOHN BARRY deceased
79 and allotted to each child as follows .. To WILLIAM BARRY one negro
man Charles and Ten pounds curt. money; To VALINDA WREN Two Negro boys and Twenty pounds currt. money .. To SARAH BARRY one negro woman and her child. June 13th 1778 .. made by WM. PAYNE, EDWD. DULIN, WM. ADAMS.
At a court held .. 15th June 1778 .. This Division was returned and ordered to be recorded.

pp. Will of ROBERT ZUILL. I ROBERT ZUILL being in perfect health ..
79- do this 22nd day of May 1776 .. at the town of Alexandria in the Colony
80 of Virginia make and publish my last will and testament .. as for my
real and personal estate which consists of my house and lott in Charles Town Cissil County in province of Maryland and a track of land on lower Machotick Creek in Colony of Virginia if recovered as it is now in suit besides what movables my wife may have in her possession ..

Now my will is that my wife, MARGARET ZUILL, take the whole of the Estate mentioned .. in trust for the maintenance and Education of my children, ELIZABETH and ROBERT ZUIELL, till they arrive to age of twenty one years then the whole to be equally divided between my children .. constitute my friend, THOMAS KIRKPATRICK, and my loving wife, MARGARET ZUILLE, Executors ..

Presence of Jas. Muir, Robert Zuille
Boy'd Reed, John Brooks,
Thomas Kirkpatrick

At a court held .. 22nd September 1778 .. will presented by MARGARET PRATT, late MARGARET ZUILLE .. admitted to record .. certificate is granted her for obtaining a probate thereof ..

pp. 80-82 Will of WILLIAM GARRET. I WILLIAM GARRET being in perfect sense and memory at this time .. give to my loving wife, MARY GARRET, all my Estate during her widowhood but in case my son, THOMAS, should arrive to age of Eighteen during my wife's widowhood then my son, THOMAS, have and enjoy as his own property two negro boys .. appoint my loving wife, MARY GARRET, THOS. LUCAS, her father, and my Father, NICHOLAS GARRET, to be Executors .. this 8th day of April 1778 (may be 18th) ..

Presence Benjn. Moody, William Garret
Timothy Carrington

At a court held .. 21st September 1778 .. will presented by THOMAS LUCAS .. admitted to record .. certificate is granted him for obtaining a probate thereof ..

pp. 82-83 Will of FLEMING PATTERSON. The last will and testament of FLEMING PATTERSON in Fairfax County .. I give unto my son, JOHN PATTERSON, 433 acres of land part of my 633 acre track on Difficult Run in Fairfax County the remainder of which I give unto my son, WILLIAM PATTERSON .. (describes how land to be laid off mentioned "where MATHEW BRADLEY formerly lived") .. I give to my son, THOMAS PATTERSON, 200 acres of land whereon I now live .. to my son, CHARLES PATTERSON, my land on Difficult Run in Loudoun County containing 157 acres .. my will is that my wife, ELIZABETH, possess my whole estate .. during her life in consideration of her bringing up and educating of the children and when the boys shall arrive to the age of Sixteen years they shall be bound out to such trades as their Mother shall think proper until they are of age. I appoint my sd wife Executrix .. this 16th day of May 1778.

Presence John Shippard, Fleming Patterson
Hugh Patterson

At a court held .. 19th October 1778 .. will presented by ELIZABETH PATTERSON .. admitted to record .. certificate is granted her for obtaining a probate thereof ..

pp. 84-85 1776. DR. The Estate of WILLIAM HARL deceased To CHARLES BROADWATER & BENJA. SEBASTIAN, Exrs. Cash recd of Edmund Sands on account of Walter English wch is due to English's administrator. CR. By John Harls Estate for Walter English's Judgment charged Wm. Harles Estate in a settlement with the Court 22d August 1752 ..

At a court held .. 22d September 1778 .. CHARLES BROADWATER, surviving Executor of WILLIAM HARL, deceased exhibited this account .. is allowed and ordered to be recorded.

pp. 84-85 1755. The Estate of JOHN HARL deceased To CHARLES BROADWATER & BENJA. SEBASTIAN. CR. By sale of your slaves Negro Bob to HUGH WEST, Woman and child to B. SEBASTIAN; old negro woman and child to HENRY GUNNELL: negro child sold GERRD. TRAMMELL ..
At a court held .. 22d Septr. 1778 .. CHARLES BROADWATER, surviving Executor of WILLIAM HARLE deceased who was administrator of JOHN HARL deceased exhibited this account .. is allowed and ordered to be recorded.

pp. 86-87 We the Subscribers met at Mr. JOHN REARDON deceased late Dwelling House & valued Inventoryed & appraised his personal estate .. items valued and totalled, £ 1667.18.0 .. given 12th October 1778 by MARTIN COCKBURN, F. ADAMS, JOHN FOWLER ..
At a court held .. 19th Octr. 1778 .. inventory returned & ordered to be recorded.

pp. 88-89 We the Subscribers do Inventory and appraise the whole of the Estate of ROBERT ZUILLE deceased that was presented to our view .. items valued and totalled, £ 95.18.0 .. given in Alexandria 14th October 1778 by appraisers JOHN CARLYLE, JOHN MUIR, JAS. MUIR ..
At a court held .. xxth Octr. 1778 .. inventory returned and ordered to be recorded.

pp. 89-90 October 27th 1778 .. we the Subscribers have valued and appraised all the Estate of WILLIAM GARRET deceased that hath been brought to our view .. items valued and totalled, £ 599.1.6 .. made by appraisers HENRY BURNAM, WILLIAM WREN, EDWARD BATES ..
At a court held .. 15th November 1778 .. inventory returned and ordered to be recorded.

pp. 90-91 A true Inventory of the Sale of the Estate of RAMOND BURNHAM deceased sold by BENJAMIN HALLY administrator 25th Feby 1778 .. no names shown except Cash received of JOHN GULLATT to be Entered to Estate ..
At a court held .. 16th November 1778 .. This sale returned and ordered to be recorded.

pp. 91-92 The Estate of RAYMOND BURNHAM deceased. 1777. To BENJAMIN HALLY administrator .. note of bond paid HENRY BURNHAM, paid WM. BURGESS account; WILLIAM GUNNELL, NANCY ROES ..
At a court held .. 16th November 1778 .. BENJAMIN HALLY administrator of the Estate of RAYMOND BURNHAM deceased exhibited this account .. is allowed and ordered to be recorded.

pp. 92-93 Will of WILLIAM BALLENGER. I do hereby leave and bequeath to my Espoused wife, MATTHEW BALLENGER (elsewhere MARTHA) my whole estate .. if she doth marry the goods and chattles to be returned to my children, JOHN BALLENGER, MARY BALLENGER, SARAH BALLENGER, JAMES BALLENGER, JACOB BALLENGER, BENJAMIN BALLENGER, KESSIA BALLENGER, they to be my heirs & that equally divided amongst them .. also I leave my wife, MATTHEW BALLENGER & my son, JOHN BALLENGER, Executors ..
Witnessed 28th July 1777 by
William Tasker, John Ballenger
William Ballenger
At a court held .. 21st Decr. 1778 .. will presented by MARTHA BALLENGER .. admitted to record .. certificate is granted her for obtaining a probate thereof ..

pp. 93-94 The Estate of DANIEL MILLS BALLENGER Deceased .. only name shown is JAS. ALVERSON. Given by CONSTANT x WILLIAMS.
At a court held .. 21st Decr. 1778 .. CONSTANT WILLIAMS admx. of the Estate of DANIEL MILLS BALLENGER deceased exhibited this account .. is allowed and ordered to be recorded.

pp. 94-95 Belvoil. Septr. 18th 1776 an Inventory of the Estate of the Revd. ANDREW MORTON deceased .. items valued but not totalled .. given by appraisers THOMAS TRIPLETT, HUMPHRY PEAKE, WM. TRIPLETT ..
At a court held .. 22nd Decr. 1778 .. inventory returned and ordered to be recorded.

pp. 96-97 1776. Estate of JOHN WARD deceased .. paid Doctor Smith; (1777) Thomas Wren, John Muir, Joseph Hodgin, Jeremiah Williams, John Fowler, John Brawner .. given by EDWARD x DAVIS. CR (1776) Cash received of Charles Little .. MARY x POPEJOY admx. of JNO. WARD.
At a court held .. 22nd Decr. 1778 .. MARY POPEJOY, admx. of Estate of JOHN WARD deceased exhibited this account .. is allowed and ordered to be recorded.

pp. 97-99 An Inventory & Appraisement of the Estate of AUGUSTUS DARRELL deceased .. mentions one horse named Lawrence .. items valued and totalled, ₤ 752.12.0 .. appraised by HUMPHRY PEAKE, ABEDNEGO ADAMS, WM. TRIPLETT ..
At a court held .. 22nd Decemr. 1778 .. inventory returned and ordered to be recorded.

pp. 99-102 Will of JOHN SPINKS. The Twenty first day of December 1778 I JOHN SPINKS of Fairfax County Planter being very sick & weak in body .. give and bequeath to my well beloved son, ROLLY SPINKS, one Feather bed & furniture, one cow & calf & Twenty pounds cash if he should ever come home to receive this Legacy .. if not his part to be equally divided among the following of my children, CHANDLER, PRESLEY, ENOCH, LINZEY and SYNTHIA .. unto my well beloved son, GERRARD SPINKS, Twenty pounds cash .. my well beloved daughter, ELIZABETH COOPER, one black horse called Indian .. my son, CHANDLER SPINKS, a certain track of land containing 166 acres lying in Prince William County for which he must pay one half the purchase money Vizt. Thirty pounds Virginia currency .. to my son, PRESLEY SPINKS, my negro boy .. to my daughters, LINZEY SPINKS & SYNTHIA SPINKS, one negro girl .. unto my son, ENOCH SPINKS, a negro girl .. my desire that my two daughters, LINZEY and SYNTHIA, may have their chests which ware given them by their Mother .. appoint my well beloved son, PRESLEY SPINKS, jointly with my Friend, RICHARD RATLIFF Executors ..
Presence Samuel Smith, John x Spinks
William Crump, Liddy x Crump,
James Connell
At a court held .. 15th February 1779 .. will presented by RICHARD RATLIFF .. admitted to record .. certificate is granted him for obtaining a probate thereof ..

pp. 102-105 We the Subscribers have appraised all the Estate of CHARLES TYLER deceased presented to our view by the administratrix .. items valued and totalled, ₤ 852.16.0 .. made 14th August 1777 by appraisers LEE MASSEY, JOHN GIBSON, WM. THOMPSON ..
At a court held .. 16th March 1779 .. inventory returned & ordered to be recorded.

pp. We the Subscribers have appraised the Estate of JOHN SPINKS de-
105- ceased & have Inventoryed the same .. items valued and totalled,
107 £ 1621.14.6 .. made by appraisers EDWD. DULIN, SAML. SMITH, JOSEPH POWELL ..
At a court held .. 19th April 1779 .. inventory returned and ordered to be recorded.

pp. We the Subscribers have appraised the Estate of WILLIAM BALLENGER
107- deceased .. items valued and totalled, £269.2.0 .. made by appraisers
109 EDWD. DULIN, EDWD. x DAVIS, DANIEL MILLS ..
At a court held .. 20th April 1779 .. inventory returned and ordered to be recorded.

pp. We the Subscribers have appraised & Inventory'd the Estate of
109- SAMUEL TALBUTT deceased in current money .. items valued and totalled,
113 £ 1578.14.11 .. of which £ 885 was the appraised value of 8 negroes .. given by appraisers JOHN HURST, JOHN WREN, ELIJA. WILLIAMS ..
At a court held .. 20th April 1779 .. inventory returned and ordered to be recorded.

pp. October 5th 1778. A Return and Accot. of the sale in amount of
113- Estate of SAMUEL TALBUTT deceased .. no purchasers mentioned .. amount
115 of sale totalled, £ 606.7.7 ..
At a court held .. 20th April 1779 .. Account of Sales returned and ordered to be recorded ..

p. Estate of SAMUEL TALBUTT deceased To MARY MAGDELANE TALBUTT, ad-
115 ministratrix .. DR. Paid John Muir, John Finley, Doctr. Wm. Belt, Mr. William Debell, Joseph Ramey, Peter Gullatt, Samuel Talbott ..
At a court held .. 20th April 1779 .. MARY M. TALBOTT administratrix of SAMUEL TALBOTT deceased exhibited this account .. is allowed and ordered to be recorded.

pp. We the Subscribers have allotted the Dower of SAMUEL TALBOTT De-
116- ceased Estate to his widow, MARY MAGDALENE TALBOTT .. items valued
117 and totalled, £ 525.9.1, of which £ 305 was the appraised value of 3 negroes .. made by appraisers JOHN WREN, JNO. HURST, ELIJA. WILLIAMS ..
At a court held .. 20th April 1779 .. Allotment of Dower returned and ordered to be recorded.

pp. Will of SAMUEL HALLEYS. The fourth day of April 1777 I SAMUEL
117- HALLEY of Fairfax County being sick and weak of body .. give and be-
119 queath to my well beloved wife, BARBERY HALLEY, all my Estate except Three negroes which my will is that she keep and enjoy them with the rest of my estate as her property during her natural life and at her death my will is that my Brother in law, WILLIAM HALLY, shall receive the 3 negroes .. if he dies before my wife my whole estate to be at disposal of my wife .. appoint my well beloved wife, BARBARY HALLEY, my Executrix ..
Presence John Ratliff, Samuel Halleys
Zachariah x Morris, George x Bozwell
At a court held .. 17th May 1779 .. will presented by BARBARA HALLY .. admitted to record .. certificate is granted her for obtaining a probate thereof ..

pp. Fairfax County. We the Subscribers have valued & appraised the
119- Estate of DANIEL TALBUT deceased .. items valued and totalled,
123 £ 943.18.0 .. given 23rd day November 1777 by appraisers GEO. MINOR,

RICHARD SANFORD, PRESLEY COX ..
At a court held .. 17th May 1779 .. inventory returned and ordered to be recorded.

pp. 123-127 Inventory of JOHN WEST JUNR. his Estate .. shows 44 negroes with an appraised value of £ 2642.10.0 .. mentions Electrical apparatus 15/ .. one sulkey harness and whip, £ 6 .. items valued and totalled, £ 3236.3.6 .. made by appraisers THOMAS TRIPLETT, GEORGE GILPIN, WM. TRIPLETT ..
At a court held .. 17th May 1779 .. inventory returned and ordered to be recorded.

pp. 128-129 The Estate of DANIEL TALBUTT deceased To ANN TALBUTT administratrix .. (1777) DR. Cash paid John Hill for nursing family smallpox; John Moss, Wm. Knight, Wm. Frazer, Elija. Williams, Miss Amelia Donaldson, John Maclocklin, John Vernon, Thomas Sinclare, Ignatious Baggett, Robert Lindsay, Wm. Adams, Wm. Gunnell for selling the Estate; received from ISAAC WREN & wife; BENJA. BOYDSTONE & wife, JOHN WREN & wife, MONICA TALBUTT, ELIZABETH TALBUTT (from each £ 111.19.10). CR. (1777) By Philip Adams, Margaret West, Benja. Talbutt, Capt. John Minor .. May 17th 1779 ..
At a court held .. 17th May 1779 .. ANN TALBUTT administratrix of DANIEL TALBUTT deceased exhibited this account .. is allowed and ordered to be recorded.

pp. 129-131 Will of CHRISTOPHER BEELER. The thirtieth day of March 1773 I CHRISTOPHER BEELER now of Hampshire County & Colony of Virginia Gent. being sick & weak in body .. give to my son, JOSEPH, Five pounds current money of Virginia & no more on account he has had more than what I am able to leave to the rest of my surviving children .. to my daughter, MARY, and her children that track of land she now lives on lying on the new Creek and the north branch in Hampshire County .. to my son, BENJAMIN, five shillings sterling he having received his full shear allready .. to my son, SAMUEL, Fifty pounds current money of Virginia over and above what I intended to leave to my grandchildren out of my house in Alexandria when sold .. to my Sister in the Cloisters in Lancaster County and in Pensylvania for taking care of my daughter, CATHARINE, when there & in her sickness in Pensylvania money the sum of one hundred pounds .. all the money my house in Alexandria will be sold for to be Divided among my grandchildren only my son, SAMUEL, to have Fifty pounds as I have ordered & the One hundred pounds to the Sisters in the Cloisters first out of the money .. not that every grandchild should have an equal part but that JOSEPH, FREDERICK, MARY, BENJAMIN & SAMUEL should be allowed no more than if the same was to be Divided amongst each of their family for some have more children than others .. make JOHN CARLYLE, JNO. DALTON who are now in partnership my Executors ..
Presence Nichs. Seaver, Christopher Beeler
John x Myars, Barbara x Myars
At a court held .. xxith June 1779 .. will presented by BENJAMIN BEELER .. admitted to record .. certificate is granted him for obtaining letters of administration with the will annexed ..

pp. 132-133 We the Subscribers have Inventory'd all the Estate of THOMAS MONROE deceased that was presented to our view .. items valued and totalled, £ 843.8.0 .. made by appraisers Humphrey Peake, Abednego Adams,

FRANCIS SUMMERS ..
At a court held .. 19th July 1779 .. inventory returned and ordered to be recorded.

pp. We the Subscribers have Inventory'd and appraised all the Estate
134- of WILLIAM PAYNE deceased that was presented to our view in current
136 money .. items valued and totalled, £ 48.6.2½ .. made September 24th
by appraisers JAMES WREN, DANIEL x MILLS, ED. DULIN ..
At a court held .. 19th July 1779 .. inventory returned and ordered to be recorded.

pp. Estate of WILLIAM PAYNE deceased .. (1776) paid Giles Cook for
136- Colo. Henry Fitzhugh, Sanfor Payne, William Tasker, Bryan Allison,
137 Ed. Payne, Jas. Richards for overlooking the plantation from August
until 13th November ..
At a court held .. 19th July 1779 .. EDWARD PAYNE, Executor of WILLIAM PAYNE deceased, exhibited this account .. is allowed and ordered to be recorded.

pp. We the Subscribers have appraised the Estate of JOHN BAITS deceased
137- & have Inventory'd the same .. mentions 70 acres of land for £ 600 ..
139 one lot of land leased, £ 200 .. items valued and totalled, £ 3014.8.0
.. given 17th July 1779 by appraisers JOHN ASKIN, CHARLES NOLAND, JAMES MOXLEY ..
At a court held .. 19th July 1779 .. inventory returned and ordered to be recorded.

pp. Inventory of the Estate of FLEMING PATTERSON as shewn us by the
139- administratrix .. items valued and totalled, £ 1038.13.7 .. appraised
143 October 22d 1778 by appraisers JOHN SHIPPERD, THOMAS GUNNELL, CHAS.
MUIRHEAD ..
At a court held .. 19th July 1779 .. inventory returned and ordered to be recorded.

pp. We the Subscribers being first duly qualified for that purpose by
143- THOMAS POLLARD Gent. have Inventory'd and appraised the Estate of
145 JOHN BOWLING deceased in current money .. items valued and totalled,
£ 574.8.0 .. given 25th Sepr. 1778 by WILLIAM ADAMS, GEO. MINOR, JOHN MOSS ..
At a court held .. 19th July 1779 .. inventory returned and ordered to be recorded.

pp. Estate of THOMAS MONROE deceased .. DR (1777). paid John Muir
145- mortgage & interest; paid John Monroe, Capt. William Ramsay, William
147 Sanford, George Minor, William Gates, John McKinsey, James Crump,
William Carlin, Thomas Dove, Joel Cooper, Thomas Kirkpatrick, Samuel McLean, Colo. George Gilpin, Colo. John Carlyle, Thomas Monroe Junr., John Fowler, Doctr. George Alexander, Bryant Allison, George Hunter, James Parsons, Richard Arell, Thomas Monroe his part of Estate as settled by Colo. George Gilpin; Francis Summers & Humphrey Peake per order of Court; do Jessey Monroe part as above; do Laurance Monroe part as above; do Catharine Monroe part; do George Monroe part; the widows 3d; balance now due to my daughter, SARAH MONROE, in my hands. CR. Sale of land sold to Mr. Hartshorn; John Moore .. August 17th 1779. CATHARINE MONROE.
At a court held .. 17th August 1779 .. CATHARINE MONROE administratrix of THOMAS MONROE deced, exhibited this accout .. is allowed and ordered to be recorded.

pp. April 25th 1778. We the Subscribers have set apart widows Dower
147- of THOMAS MONROES Estate and Divided the said Estate among the said
149 Decedents children Vizt. the widows thirds then THOMAS MONROE, JESSEY MONROE, LAWRANCE MONROE, CATY MONROE, GEORGE MONROE & SARAH MONROE .. the estate if £ 1967.9.8, deduct for debt, £ 916.17.0; Divided £ 1050. 12.8 .. (each legatees' part is broken down) .. made by GEORGE GILPIN, FRANCIS SUMMERS, HUMPHREY PEAKE ..

At a court held .. 17th August 1779 .. Division was returned and ordered to be recorded.

p. Estate of SARAH MOSS to Executor. (1778) DR. LIDIA HALBERT one
149 bed and furniture; THOMAS BEACH, MASSON JOHNSON, WM. DULIN, JOHN DULIN, ED. DULIN, SAMUEL SMITH, DRAKEFORD GRAY .. 16th August 1779 .. EDWD. DULIN ..

At a court held .. xxth Septr. 1779 .. EDWARD DULIN exhibited this account .. is allowed and ordered to be recorded.

pp. Estate of THOMAS MOSS deceased to EDWD. DULIN Executor. DR. (1778)
150- .. to Mr. John Mercer for coffin; Mr. Richard Magers for Funeral Ser-
152 mon; Mason Johnson; Ann Goatlys Legacy; John Goatlys Legacy; Francis Hall for weaving; Doctr. Smith; Jane Langley; Jno. ODaniel; Saml. Smith; Mary Halbert; Abraham Beach; Danl. Jenkins; Philip Grimes; John Moss; Wm. Moss; Robert Moss; Thos. Moss (each of these four £ 478.9.6) .. James Dove, John Dulin, Sarah Moss part of Deced Estate £ 2113.5.6 .. Palmer Hall; Capt. John Wren for appraising; Drummond Wheeler for appraising Tobacco. Contra. Alexr. Roe; Robt. McDugal; Jane Langley; Wm. D. Bell; Henry Burnham; Mason Johnson; Ann Goatly Legacy; Sarah Mosses part of the Debt; mistake in acct of Elija. Williams, Colo. Masons Rent .. 16th August 1779, EDWD. DULIN, Executor ..

At a court held .. xxth Septr. 1779 .. EDWARD DULIN exhibited this account .. is allowed and ordered to be recorded.

p. We the Subscribers have Inventoryed and appraised all the Estate
152 of WILLIAM BRONAUGH deceased that was presented to our view .. (a cow, hogs and two shoats) .. items valued and totalled, £ 7.14.0 .. made by appraisers ROBERT BOGGESS, GILBERT SIMPSON, WILLIAM BAYLEY ..

At a court held .. 18th Octo. 1779 .. inventory returned and ordered to be recorded.

pp. Will of PHILIP MASON. I PHILIP MASON of county of Fairfax and
152- Parish of Fairfax being in perfect sence and memory .. will and desire
153 my lands in Prince William County be sold and my wife, LETICE MASON, to receive the third part of the money and ROBERT MASEY the residue. The remaining part of my estate I give to my wife, LETICE MASON, during her life or widowhood and then to be divided between my five children. Desire that after my wife's death the plantation where I now live be equally divided between my two sons, DANIEL JENKINS or MASON and NATHANIEL MASON, during the term of the Lease.. I give my two children, PHILIP MASON and FRANCIS MASON, twenty shillings each if they ever call for it. I appoint my wife, LETICE MASON, my Executor .. this 28th day of July 1779 ..

Presence of John Jackson, Philip Mason

Letice x Deakins, Frances x Bates

At a court held .. 15th Novemr. 1779 .. will proved and ordered to be recorded.

p. 154 1779. WILLIAM BRONAUGH Deced To WM. REARDON Exr. Dr. Cash paid on bond to JOHN GIBSON; CHARLES MOLOHON ..

At a court held .. 16th Novr. 1779 .. WILLIAM REARDON, Admr. of WILLIAM BRONAUGH deceased exhibited this account .. is allowed and ordered to be recorded.

pp. 154-155 Will of LAWRENCE HOUGH. I LAWRENCE HOUGH the Elder of the Town of Alexandria in the county of Fairfax being weak in body .. give and bequeath to my Loving wife, MARGERET HOUGH, during her natural life and to be disposed of at her death among my children in such division as may seem meet to her .. appoint my loving wife, MARGERET HOUGH, my Executrix .. this 5th day of August 1776.

Presence John Orr, Lawrence Hough
Peter Wise, Cunrod Doyle

At a court held .. 18th Novr. 1779 .. will presented by MARGRET HOUGH .. admitted to record .. certificate is granted her for obtaining a probate thereof ..

pp. 155-157 Will of THOMAS BAYLISS. I THOMAS BAYLISS of Parish of Truro in county of Fairfax do make this my last will and testament .. it is my will that the plantation whereon I now live be sold at Publick sale .. money arising to be apply'd towards the payment of my just debts. The rest of my Estate of any kind be equally divided between my loving wife, MARTHA ROLLINGS BAYLISS, and my six children vizt. WILLIAM PAYNE BAYLISS, THOMAS BAYLISS, EDWARD JONES BAYLISS, SARAH JOHNSON, ALICI TAWS and ELENOR MILLER .. provided she (his wife) stands to this my will and if she refuses .. is to have what the Law will allow her and no more. My desire that after my Estate be equally divided into seven parts by DANIEL McCARTY, RICHARD CHICHESTER and THOMAS TRIPLETT that my son, WILLIAM PAYNE BAYLISS, have his first choice, my son, THOMAS BAYLISS, to have second choice and my son, EDWARD JONES BAYLISS, to have third choice, my wife, MARTHA ROLLINGS BAYLISS, to have fourth choice, my daughter, SARAH JOHNSON, to have fifth choice, my daughter, ALICI TAWS, to have sixth choice and my daughter, ELENER MILLER to have the seventh choice. I appoint my two sons, WILLIAM PAYNE BAYLISS and THOMAS BAYLISS, my Exrs. .. this first day of December 1779 ..

Presence Daniel McCarty, Thomas Bayliss
Charles x Beach, John x Johnson

At a court held .. 21st February 1780 .. will presented by WILLIAM PAYNE BAYLISS and THOMAS BAYLISS .. admitted to record .. certificate is granted them for obtatining a probate thereof ..

pp. 157-159 Will of JOHN MINOR. I JOHN MINOR of County of Fairfax & Parish of Fairfax being low in health .. give and bequeath to my daughter, JEAN SANFORD MINOR, one negro girl to be delivered to her at the day of marriage or at Eighteen years of age .. to my son, JOHN MINOR, one negro boy .. to my daughter, MARCIA, one negro girl (same conditions as Jean) .. unto my well beloved wife, ANN MINOR, all the rest of my Estate during her natural life or widowhood .. in case (she) should marry my will is that my Exrs. should take the Estate and divide it between my three children before mentioned .. appoint my well beloved wife, ANN MINOR, and JOHN MOSS and GEORGE MINOR my Executors .. this 14th day March 1779 ..

Presence Thomas Darn, John Minor
John x Davis, Ann x Davis

At a court held .. 21st Febry. 1780 .. will presented by ANN MINOR .. admitted to record .. certificate granted her for obtaining a probate ..

pp. 159-162 Will of GERRARD BOWLING. I GERRARD BOWLING of Fairfax County being sick & weak .. give and bequeath to my son, GERRARD BOWLING, slaves (3 named) .. unto my son, SIMON BOWLING (3 slaves).. to my son, SAMUEL BOWLING (3 slaves) .. to my son, ROBERT BOWLING (3 slaves) .. (each son also given cattle, sheep, furniture) .. to my daughter JEAN BOWLING, two slaves .. to my daughter, ANN WISE, a negro girl now in the possession of her husband, PETER WISE .. unto my daughter, LOUISIANA RATLIFF, a negro girl now in possession of her husband, RICHARD RATLIFF .. to my wife after she takes the thirds of my Estate .. all the rest of my Estate .. for the support of herself and my two young sons, SAMUEL and ROBERT, until they arrive to age of Twenty one years .. if my wife does not marry again .. the rest of my estate shall after her decease be equally divided between my four sons, GERRARD, SIMON, SAMUEL & ROBERT .. appoint my wife and my two sons, GERRARD & SIMON, Executors .. this 29th day December 1779 ..

Presence Charles Alexander, Osburn Talburt, Levi Talburt — Gerrard x Bowling

At a court held .. 21st February 1780 .. will proved and ordered to be recorded.

pp. 162-164 Will of HARRY PIPER. I HARRY PIPER of Town of Alexandria Merchant being in good health .. do this 21st day of November 1774 make & publish my last will and testament .. I give to my Sister, ELIZABETH SARGENT, Four hundred pounds sterling .. if she dies before will takes effect to be equally divided among her children .. to my Sister, JEAN WALKER (the wife of WILLIAM WALKER), Four hundred pounds sterling .. if she dies before will takes effect to be equally divided among her children. I give to Miss MARY DIXON, the daughter of my friend, JOHN DIXON Esqr., One hundred pounds sterling. I give to Miss BETTY RAMSAY Twenty five pounds sterling .. to Miss SARAH MASTERSON Twenty five pounds sterling .. to my God son, WILLIAM RAMSAY, Twenty five pounds sterling .. to my God daughter, SALLY HARRISON, Twenty five pounds sterling also a right to a third part of a pew in the Church at Alexandria now the property of JOHN MUIR, WILLIAM RAMSAY & myself; as a small token of my friendship for my relation JOHN DIXON Esqr. I hope he will accept my gold watch. My faithful servant, CHARLES, hath served me long & I hope from my treatment of him during the time of his servitude he has seldom had reason to feel the pain of his being a slave and advise fortune may go hard with him, therefore it is my will .. he be set free. It is not convenient for me to comply with the laws of this Colony prescribed for setting of slaves Free, yet I hope while he continues to behave well, if he chuses it, he may still live in this Colony unmolested but if there should be any danger of his being taken up & sold, it is my hope I shall have some Friends left to interfer in his behealf, it is my desire if that should be the case that he may be sent to England or any other place he may chuse where he can be Free & the Expence of his Passage to be paid by my Exrs. If I shall die at Mr. Ramsays in Alexandria, I desire that Ten pounds may be given to the House servants to be divided by Mrs. Ramsay. I bequeath unto my Brother, ANTHONY PIPER, all the residue of my Estate. I constitute my Brother, ANTHONY PIPER, & request my good Friend, JOHN DIXON Esqr. will join him as Executor ..

(No witnesses shown.) — Harry Piper

At a court held .. 22d Feby. 1780 .. WILLIAM RAMSAY and JOHN MUIR presented this instrument of writing and made oath they found the same among the papers of HARRY PIPER deceased .. on their motion is ordered to be recorded.

pp. 164-168 1778. The Estate of JOHN WEST JUNR. Deced To THOMAS WEST .. paid THOMAS NEALE for two pr. Waggon wheels; PETER WISE for side Leather; JOHN & GEORGE FOWLERS acct. agt. my Fathers Estate; HORN, wheelright for mending cart; JOHN VERNON for making shoes; PHILIP CLELAND for weaving; JOHN FRAZER for butning a Coat; THOMAS JOHNSON for weaving; JAMES HALLEY, WILLIAM BARNARDS acct agt the Estate; LEWIS WESTON for one pair of shoes; Mr. ARELL to defend a suit by rose against West & Little. Contra. Recd of Mr. Charles Little; sold Lawrence Hoof 5 small Beeves, John Rhodes; balance due Estate from THOS. WEST manager.

At a court held .. 21st March 1780 .. THOMAS WEST one of the Executors of JOHN WEST JUNR. deceased exhibited this accot .. is allowed and ordered to be recorded.

pp. 169-170 1779. Estate of JOHN WEST Esqr. deceas'd To Acct with CHARLES LITTLE .. to JOHN WEST JUNIOR deceased; JOHN WEST Younger; HUGH WEST; Miss CATHARINE WEST, Miss FRANCINA WEST, Miss SALLY WEST. Contra. John Peake. Above accot proved by CHARLES LITTLE Decr. 20th 1779 before JOHN CARLYLE.

At a court held .. 21st March 1780 .. CHARLES LITTLE exhibited this account against the Estate of JOHN WEST JUNR. deced .. is allowed and ordered to be recorded.

pp. 170-172 1778. Mr. JOHN WEST To THOMAS WEST. DR. Francis Summers, paid Mr. Anderson for your board when learning Navigation with Connelly.

1778. Miss KITTY WEST to THOMAS WEST. DR. Hair comb, paper pins, pair gloves, thread, to Duncan for making you a pair of silk shoes, 7½ yards Linnen, 8 hanks of Sewing Silk.

1778. Miss FRANCES WEST to THOMAS WEST. DR. Paper pins, 1 hatt cost £ 6, one pair of shoes ..

1778. Miss SARAH WEST to THOMAS WEST. DR. for one Paper pins, one hair comb, pair of shoes, cash paid John Vernon for making you shoes ..

1779. Mr. HUGH WEST to THOMAS WEST. DR. Trimmings for your coat, making one pair shoes ..

At a court held .. 21st March 1780 .. THOMAS WEST exhibited accounts against the children of JOHN WEST JUNR. deceased .. is allowed and ordered to be recorded.

pp. 172-174 Fairfax County to wit. We the Subscribers do Inventory and appraise all the Estate of THOMAS BAYLIS deced which was presented to our view .. items valued and totalled, £ 6397.0.0 .. (inventory shows one Negro woman appraised at £ 2500, one Negro girl at £ 1800 and one Negro child at £ 200) .. given 29th February 1780 by appraisers RICHARD CHICHESTER, THOMAS TRIPLETT, WILLIAM TRIPLETT.

(No recording date.)

pp. 175-176 The Estate of CHARLES TURNER deced To ROBERT MUIR Administrator. DR. 1776. Josiah Watson, Isaac Gostling, Elenor Evans, John Allison, John Stone, Doctr. Wm. Rumney, Molly Shaw for washing dirty cloathes before the sale, Mary Saunders, John Chew, Burrows Dowdney, William McKnight, Colin Dunlop & Sons & Company, William Hunter, Thomas Kirkpatrick, Henry Shaffer. Contra. (1776) cash from Thomas Conway (March 21st), John Luke, Sampson Turley, Thomas Armatt, James Taylor, Wm. Hunter (on acct of Wm. Wilson), Peter Wagener, George Gilpin, William Smith, Joseph Speake .. save Errors ROBERT MUIR, Alexandria 10th June 1780.

At a court held .. 20th June 1780 .. ROBERT MUIR, administrator of CHARLES TURNER deceased, exhibited this account .. is allowed and ordered to be recorded.

(Error in page numbering. There are no pages numbered 181 through 190.)

pp. 176-191 Alexandria April 22d 1776. An account of sales of the Effects of CHARLES TURNER deceased .. purchasers James Wren, Richard Conway, William Carlin, Michael Gretter, Alexander Chisholm, Samuel Smith, Moses Ball, Thomas Fleming, Roger Chew, Edward Owens, Andrew Wayles, Edward Sanford, Robert Muir, Burrows Dowdney, John Nevil, Philip Daw, Philip Jackson, Thomas Crafts, Peter Wise, William Hunter Junr., John Sanford, Robert Adam, William Paton, Adam Lynn, William Bushby, Tobias Zimmerman, Samuel McLean, Benjamin Moody, John Orr, Thomas Sinclair, John Thorn, James Parsons, Colo. John Carlyle, William Mountjoy, John Chew, John Dalton, James Connell, Alexander Pierce, John Shaw, John Philips, Isaac Gostling, William McKnight, Thomas Kirkpatrick, William Brown ..

At a court held .. 20th June 1780 .. account of sales was returned and ordered to be recorded.

pp. 191-196 An inventory and appraisement of the Estate of CHARLES TURNER deceased taken by JAMES KIRK, HARRY PIPER & JAMES CONNELL .. items valued and totalled, £ 377.3.6 .. includes servant named William Villele ..

At a court held .. 20th June 1780 .. inventory returned and ordered to be recorded.

pp. 196-197 Will of JAMES MUIR. I JAMES MUIR being in a weake state of health .. my Executors pay two thirds to my Father, Mother & Brother if they are alive, if the law will not permit them to have it, or should they be dead, I then leave the same to my Executor .. the other one third to my God Son, ROBERT ADAM MARTAIN, as he is the only one I ever had .. appoint my worthy Friend, ROBERT ADAM Esqr. my Executor .. will written by myself this 26th day of June 1780.

Witness William Hepburn, Jas. Muir

Lawrence Hooff, R. (Richard) M. Gerrard

At a court held .. 22nd August 1780 .. will presented by ROBERT ADAM .. admitted to record .. certificate is granted him for obtaining a probate thereof ..

pp. 197-199 1777. Estate of THOMAS SHAW Deceased .. DR. Cash paid William Frazer, Wm. Payne sheriff, Wm. Bushby, Richard Gerrard, John Hough for quit rents, Roger Chew for coffin, William McKnight for do, Jonathan Thomas, John Bridges, James Muir, William Brown, John Minor, John Muir, Charles Gerrard, Doctr. Smith, William Gerrard, Jenny Dalton, Robert Muir for Miss Daltons, Henry Wishearts estate, legacy to Jemima Minor. Contra. (1777). Cash received of Robert Muir, John Bridges, Rachael Savage, John Thomas's rent ..

At a court held .. 22nd Augt. 1780 .. GEORGE MINOR, Executor of THOMAS SHAW, deceased exhibited this account .. is allowed and ordered to be recorded.

p. 200 Inventory of the Estate of JOHN PETTOTH (also shown as PETTIT) Deceased .. items valued and totalled, £ 79.17.11 .. made by appraisers JOHN BARRY, JAMES BROWN, DANIEL STONE.
July Court 1777. Inventory returned and ordered to be recorded.

p. 201 ROBERT DOUGLASS To the Estate of JOHN PETTIT Deceased. Mentions widows Dower with whom ROBT. DOUGLASS intermarried ..
At a court held .. 22nd Augt. 1780 .. ROBERT DOUGLASS admr. of JOHN PETTIT deceased exhibited this account .. is allowed and ordered to be recorded.

pp. 201-203 We the Subscribers being first duly qualified by GEORGE GILPIN Gent. have Inventoried and appraised the Estate of SAMUEL HAWLEY deceased in current money .. items valued and totalled £ 2913.9.0 .. given 16th day July 1779 by JOHN MOSS, JOHN RATCLIFF, RICHD. RATCLIFF ..
At a court held .. 18th September 1780 .. inventory returned and ordered to be recorded.

pp. 203-207 Will of JOHN CARLYLE. I JOHN CARLYLE of Town of Alexandria in county of Fairfax and State of Virginia being of sound & disposing mind & memory do make this my last will and testament .. and as to my body I desire it may be intered under the Tombstone in the enclosed ground in the Presbyterian Yard near where my first wife and children are intered. I give & devise to my Grandson, CARLYLE FAIRFAX WHITING, my Track of land in Berkley County called Limekills or the neck on the Potomack River near the mouth of Opeckon Creek .. also the half of my moiety of a Track of land in Culpepper County containing 1524 acres patented in the name of GEO. WILLIAM FAIRFAX & his sister, SARAH, my first wife. GEO. WM. FAIRFAX made me deeds for his part to me & my heirs. I also give my said Grandson, CARLYLE FAIRFAX WHITING, a part of my two Lotts whereon I live in Alexandria beginning on Cameron & Water street at the corner thence extending on Cameron Street .. then parallel to Fairfax Street .. also one fourth part of my land taken out of the River adjoining Mr. Ramsay .. (if he dies without issue) to my grandson, JOHN CARLYLE HERBERT .. rents and profits of lands devised to my grandson, CARLYLE FAIRFAX WHITING, be applyed to his Education and support until he comes of age .. also to my grandson, CARLYLE FAIRFAX WHITING, Five hundred pounds when he comes to age of twenty one years. I give and devise to my daughter, SARAH HERBERT, my other moiety or one fourth part of the Track of land in Culpeper Cy containing 1524 acres as described above .. also a part of my Lott whereon I live .. unto my grandson, JOHN CARLYLE HERBERT, Five hundred pounds to be paid him when he comes to age twenty one years. I give unto my Couzen, CHARLES LITTLE, Five hundred pounds to be paid him as soon after my death as my Estate can spare the money & request that he would take charge & management of my Estate until my Son comes of age .. I bequeath the Interest of Five hundred pounds to the Poor of the Presbyterian Society in or near Alexandria .. devise all the rest of my Estate unto my son, GEORGE WILLIAM CARLYLE .. in case he dies before age twenty one years without issue, I desire my said Estate to my grandson, JOHN CARLYLE HERBERT and CARLYLE FAIRFAX WHITING .. my most Earnest request to my Executors to pay a particular regard to the Education of my son .. appoint my son in law, WILLIAM HERBERT, my Couzen, Mr. CHARLES LITTLE, my Friend, Mr. WILLIAM ELLZEY & ROBERT McCREA, Executors .. my friend, Mr. ELLZEY, has promised his care of

my Estate as he knows more of it than any other person living .. once more beg that particular attention be paid to the Education of my son. I would wish him to be kept with Mr. BOOTH or at the best place for Education that can be got & not regard the expence .. each of my Executors accept the small sum of Ten pounds .. this 5th day April 1780.
John Carlyle
All in my own handwriting - John Carlyle.
At a court held .. 17th Octr. 1780 .. will presented by WILLIAM HERBERT & CHARLES LITTLE .. admitted to record .. certificate granted them for obtaining a probate thereof ..

pp. List of the Account paid by Capt. SAMPSON DARRELL and the Widow of
207- the said Capt. SAMPSON DARRELL since the decease of the above Capt.
208 SAMPSON DARRELL for account of GUSTAVUS DARRELL deceased vizt. 1777. To Andrew Wales, (1778) John Graham, John & Geo. Fowler, John McKinsey, William Rumney, Henry Biggs for Catharine Blinstone, Thomas Barker, Thomas Munroe, Elisha & Thomas Baily, William Hunter Senr., Wm. Cohagan, Sampson Dorrell, John Wiley, Randolph Biggs, Christopher Shields, Jas. McDonald, John McFarland, Bryant Allison, Kezial Williams. As per receipt delivered to October Court 1780.
At a court held .. 17th October 1780 .. MARY DARRELL widow and relict of SAMPSON DARRELL deced who was Exor. of AUGUSTUS DARRELL deceased exhibited this account .. is allowed and ordered to be recorded.

pp. We whose names are underwritten have valued and appraised all the
208- Estate and Effects of MOSES SIMPSON deceased .. items valued and to-
209 talled, £ 3153.3.8 .. Octr. 15th 1779 .. made by appraisers FRANCIS COFFER, JOHN TILLET, THOMAS SONGSTER. A true account of the amount of the sale of the above articles, £ 1839.12.6 the Sale being in October 22d 1779, Novr. 5th do & Feby 5th 1780. GEORGE SIMPSON.
At a court held .. 17th Octr. 1780 .. inventory returned and ordered to be recorded.

pp. An Inventory of Capt. THOMAS TRIPLETT Estate Real & Personal Octo-
209- ber 24th 1780 .. includes 14 slaves with appraised value of £ 25,400 ..
214 items valued and totalled, £ 61,760.0.0 .. made by appraisers CHARLES LITTLE, HUMPHREY PEAKE, ABEDNEGO ADAMS.
At a court held .. xxth Novr. 1780 .. inventory returned and ordered to be recorded.

pp. We the Subscribers have appraised the Estate of JOHN STONE deceased
214- & have Inventoried the same .. items valued and totalled, £ 132.8.5 ..
215 made 18th day November 1780 by appraisers RICHD. RATCLIFF, ISAAC DAVIS, JOHN ASKIN.
At a court held .. 20th November 1780 .. inventory returned and ordered to be recorded.

pp. An Inventory of the Estate of THOMAS HALBERT Deceased .. items
215- valued and totalled, £ 1283.10.0 .. made by appraisers WILLIAM STONE,
217 DRUMMOND WHEELER, JOHN ASKIN.
At a court held .. 20th Novr. 1780 .. inventory returned and ordered to be recorded.

pp. The Inventory of Mrs. CATHARINE MONROE Deceased Estate sold by
217- Order of Court 31st of May 1778 by the Sheriff .. paid Robt. Sanford
219 for removing the goods from the plantation to Francis Summers .. pur-

chasers .. Caty Monroe, Benja. Clark Payne, George Minor, William Payne, Hugh Middleton, Charles Gerrard, Capt. Thomas West, William Mills, Daniel Donaldson, Samuel Johnson, Robert Sanford, Lewis Hipkins, Francis Summers, John Ellis, William Crump, William Bushby, Robert Harper, Thomas Sinclair. Hector Ross, Sheriff.

At a court held .. 21st November 1780 .. William Payne late Sheriff who was ordered to sell the Estate of CATHARINE MONROE deceased exhibited this account .. ordered to be recorded, to which account and Judgment of the said Court the representative of CATHARINE MONROE objected as there was no voucher produced to support the charges contained in the account but the Court over ruled the objection and allowed the account to be recorded upon the said WILLIAM PAYNE proveing the accounts to be just and true by his own oath.

pp. 219-220 Know all men .. we ROBERT POWELL, MARGARET WEST, CHARLES LITTLE & PETER WAGENER are bound unto WILLIAM RAMSAY, JAMES HENDRICKS, ROBERT McCREA, JOSIAH WATSON & GEORGE GILPIN Gentlemen Justices of the County Court of Fairfax .. in sum of Five Hundred thousand pounds current money of Virginia .. 25th November 1780. Condition .. if ROBERT POWELL & MARGARET WEST, guardians of ROGER WEST .. shall pay unto the said orphan all such estates as now is or hereafter shall come to (their) possession .. obligation to be void ..

Robt. Powell Charles Little
Margt. West Pet. Wagener

At a court held .. 21st Novr. 1780 .. Bond acknowledged and ordered to be recorded.

p. 221 An Inventory of JERRARD BOLLINGS JUNIORS Estate taken & appraised by us in old money this 14th of Decr. 1780 .. items valued and totalled, £ 99.5.6 .. made by appraisers PHILIP ALEXANDER, WILLIAM BOLING, OSBORN TALBERT.

At a court held .. 16th January 1781 .. inventory returned & ordered to be recorded.

pp. 221-222 An Inventory of GERARD BOLLINGS Estate taken and appraised by us in old money with an allowance of Forty for one this 19th day October 1780 .. items valued and totalled, £ 32,768 .. made by appraisers OSBORN TALBERT, ROBERT ADAM, PHILIP ALEXANDER ..

At a court held .. 16th Jany 1781 .. inventory returned and ordered to be recorded.

p. 222 Agreeable to the within order we have divided the real estate of MOSES SIMPSON deced and have aloted Negro Clo to the Widows dower by paying Thirteen pounds Specie and the residue to the orphin .. FRANCIS COFFER, THOS. SANGSTER, JOHN TILLETT ..

To the most Honourable Court in Fairfax County. Whereas this comes to acquaint you that I have received the alotment made by Capt. Cofer & Thomas Songster & John Tillett in my deceased Husbands Estate. February 19th 1781, MARGRET x SIMPSON. Test. Sarah x Windsor, Aaron Simpson.

At a court held .. 20th March 1781 .. This receipt & allotment returned and ordered to be recorded.

pp. 223-224 FRANCIS MASON orph. to Mr. JOHN REARDON deceased. 1768. DR. 1 boys hatt, 1 pair shoes, 1 years board .. (1769) making 1 sute of clothes, 1 stick of twist, 1 dozen buttons, 2 pair shoes, 1 felt hatt,

1 years board,.. (1770) 4 yds of linen, 3½ yds of white, 1 felt hatt, 2 yds Irish linen, 4 yds of Cambrick, 1 pair of shoe buckles, 1½ yds of duffella, making coat & breeches, 1 yrs board .. (1771) 1 year & 9 months schooling, 1 spelling book, 1 Felt hatt, 1 years board .. (1772) cloathing and board .. (1773) cloathing and board .. (1774) cloathing and board (same for years 1775 through 1778) .. (1779) cloathing and board 8½ months. Contra shows income from 1103 pounds of Tobacco for the years 1768-1778. Debits exceeded income of Estate.

At a court held .. 21st May 1781 .. ANN DONALDSON administratrix of JOHN REARDON deceased who was appointed guardian to FRANCIS MASON exhibited this account .. is allowed and ordered to be recorded.

pp. 224-225 Inventory of Estate of PHILIP MASON deceased taken by JOHN JACKSON, JOHN SHORTRIDGE & WILLIAM SCOTT who were appointed to appraise the said Estate .. items valued and totalled, £ 3179.4.0 .. given 5th day August 1780 ..

At a court held .. 21st May 1781 .. inventory returned and ordered to be recorded.

pp. 225-226 The Estate of Capt. JOHN WEST deced in account with the Executors .. DR. Cash paid Capt. Charles Little, Capt. Thomas West, Capt. Benjamin Clarke Payne for selling the Estate at Cameron, Mrs. Sybil West for the use of her plantation house, plantation utensils & house furniture from the year 1771 to the year 1780 inclusive pursuant to the reservation made by the said Sybil when she gave up the possession of them to Capt. JOHN WEST, paid THOMAS WEST his Dividend of the Estate, paid BALDWIN DADE his dividend due his Lady, paid JOHN WEST his dividend, paid HUGH WEST his dividend, paid FRANCINA WEST her dividend, paid SARAH WEST her dividend .. (each £ 8126.7.8 3/4) .. examined by JOSIAH WATSON and JAMES HENDRICKS 22d May 1781.

At a court held .. 23d May 1781 .. GEORGE WEST one of the Executors of JOHN WEST JUNR. deceased exhibited this account .. is allowed and ordered to be recorded.

pp. 226-227 An Account of the Sales of the personal estate of JOHN WEST JUNR. deced which was sold by order of the commissioners appointed to make a division of the Estate among his children .. purchasers .. Capt. Benja. Clarke Payne, Robert Harper, John Gretter, Wm. Scott, Capt. Baldwin Dade, Wm. Bowling, John West, Wm. Linday, Roger West, Wm. Keating, William Payne, Capt. Thomas West, Capt. Little for himself & the 3 younger children, Charles Jones, William Ward, Thomas Fleming .. the total £ 8181.9.0 ..

At a court held .. 22d May 1781 .. This account of sales returned and ordered to be recorded.

pp. 227-233 DR. Capt. THOMAS WEST in account with the Executors of JOHN WEST deceased .. cash paid your guardian, Capt. THOMAS WEST .. examined by same ..

DR. Mr. HUGH WEST in account with Executors of JOHN WEST deceased .. paid Capt Little his account against you, paid Capt. THOMAS WEST his account against you; sundry accounts delivered your guardian, Mr. CHARLES JONES, to collect; your part of the sales of the personal estate of HUGH, FRANCINA and SARAH WEST; by one third of Mrs. WESTS charge agt. yr fathers estate for rent which was paid by you & yr Sisters, FRANCINA & SARAH .. examined by same ..

DR. Capt. BALDWIN DADE in account with the Executors of JOHN WEST decd .. paid Capt. CHARLES LITTLE his account against your Lady .. examined by same ..
DR. Miss SARAH WEST in account with Executors of JOHN WEST deced .. cash paid your guardian, Capt. THOMAS WEST .. examined by same ..
DR. Miss FRANCINA WEST in account with Executors of JOHN WEST deced .. paid your guardian, Capt. BALDWIN DADE .. examined by same ..
DR. Estate of HUGH WEST, FRANCINA WEST and SARAH WEST in account with JOHN WESTS Executors .. examined by same ..

An account of the sales of the personal Effects of HUGH WEST, FRANCINA WEST and SARAH WEST .. purchasers William Boling, Thomas West, Charles Little, Colo. Gilpin, John Gretter, William Hunter, Michael Gretter, Hugh West, Baldwin Dade, William Ward, Robert Sanford, Charles Jones, Peter Wise, John Grayham, Francis Summers, Charles Jerrard ..

(No recording date.)

p. 233 Miss CHARLOTTE WISHEART in account with WILLIAM SIMPSON guardian .. June 1778 .. your part in payment of WM. ELLZEY for taking the estate of your deceased father out of Colo. Carlyles hands; your part for petitioning the bench for administration of said Estate; paid JOHN CARLYLE Exr. of JOHN DALTON deceased, paid GEORGE MINER for 5 months board; for provisions & Clothing for Soldier ..

At a court held .. 21st August 1781 .. WILLIAM SIMPSON guardian to CHARLOTTE WISHEART exhibited this account .. is allowed and ordered to be recorded.

pp. 233-234 Will of BENJAMIN CHAPIN. I BENJAMIN CHAPIN of Town of Alexandria, Surgeon, being infirm in body .. give and bequeath unto my well beloved wife, MARGARET CHAPIN, all my Estate (except what is hereinafter excepted) .. until such time as my youngest daughter, MARGARET, shall arrive unto the full age of Eighteen years at which time it is my will that my sons, HIRAM & GURDEN, do have my house and lott in Alexandria equally divided between them the third part excepted & reserved unto their Mother during her life .. (if my wife does not live until MARGARET arrives to age) .. my sons, HIRAM & GURDEN, do have the said house and lott allowing my daughters, ELIZABETH, ANN and MARGARET, a full third part of the profits thereof .. what was herein before excepted is a lott and house I have in Town of New London and State of Connecticut which I give to my sons to be equally divided among them at the time GURDEN arrives to age of twenty one years .. appoint my true & trusty friend, MICHAEL THORN, of town & county aforesaid Executor and my well beloved wife, MARGARET CHAPIN, Executrix .. this 13th day of August 1781.

Presence Jacob Cox, Benja. Chapin
Oliver Price, Washer Blunt

At a court held .. 15th October 1781 .. will presented by MARGARET CHAPIN and MICHAEL THORN .. admitted to record .. certificate is granted them for obtaining a probate thereof ..

pp. 234-235 Will of TOWNSHEND DADE. I TOWNSHEND DADE the Elder of Fairfax County Gent. being sick and weak in body .. give and bequeath all my slaves and personal estate to my wife, PARTHENIA DADE .. after her decease the same be equally divided between my two married daughters, ANN WEST and SARAH TRIPLETT, my unmarried daughter being already pro-

vided for by a Deed of Conveyance executed by me and my wife, and my son, TOWNSHEND DADE, having received from me a good Education which is all the fortune I am able to give him and much greater than any of my other children will receive. I appoint my said wife Executrix .. this 21st day February 1777.
Presence Lee Massey, Towsh'd Dade
Charles Little, Francis Alexander
At a court held .. 15th October 1781 .. will proved .. admitted to record.

pp. 235-236 Will of JAMES STEUART. I JAMES STEUART of Town of Alexandria .. give and devise unto my wife, BETTY STEUART, the use of one half of my real and personal Estate during her life. I give and devise all the rest & residue of my Estate to my son, WILLIAM RAMSAY STEUART, and the child with which my wife is now pregnant .. after the death of my wife, the part which she has the use of in like manner .. appoint WILLIAM RAMSAY, DENNIS RAMSAY & HUGH STEUART Executors .. this 28th day of October 1781.
Presence Jas. Keith, James Steuart
Wm. Herbert, Sarah Masterson
At a court held .. 20th November 1781 .. will presented by WILLIAM RAMSAY and DENNIS RAMSAY .. admitted to record .. certificate is granted them for obtaining a probate thereof ..

pp. 236-237 Will of WILLIAM HARDEN. I WILLIAM HARDEN do give and bequeath unto my loving wife, STACY, 300 acres of land adjoining the plantation whereon I now live, likewise five negroes .. half the stock .. during her natural life then to my well beloved son, THOMAS GREEN HARDEN .. (other bequests) .. in case THOMAS GREEN HARDEN dies without heirs .. the land to become the property of my son, CHARLES .. to my well beloved son, HALL HARDEN, a piece of land part of the tract whereon I now live .. unto my well beloved daughter, MARYAN BALL, 100 acres of land .. to my son, CHARLES, four negroes .. also the leased plantation during the term of years he now lives on .. unto my son, ANTHONY, three negroes with the leased plantation where he now lives .. unto ALEXANDER WILLIAM'S children and each of them a cow & calf, one sow and pigs, one Ewe and lamb. I likewise give MARTHA HARDEN'S children and each of them (the same). The above stock comes out of CHARLES and ANTHONY HARDENS estate equally .. this 18th day of May 1781.
Presence Joseph Birch, W. Carlin
William x Harden
Executors JOSEPH BIRCH, CHARLES CRAY, CHARLES HARDING.
At a court held .. 16th October 1781 .. will proved by (witnesses) and JOHN BOLLING made oath he heard the Testator direct JOSEPH BIRCH who wrote the will alter the device to his wife, STACY, from one third to half of his Stock which was ordered to be recorded ..
and at a Court held .. xixth day November in the year aforesaid administration with will annexed was granted CHARLES HARDEN .. certificate was granted him for obtaining letters of administration ..

pp. 237-239 We the Subscribers appraised the Estate of WILLIAM HARDEN Deceased .. items valued and totalled, £ 611.10.10 .. made by appraisers WM. ADAMS, JAMES HURST, ALLEN DAVIES ..
At a court held .. 22nd Jany 1782 .. inventory returned and ordered to be recorded.

pp. 239-240 We the Subscribers have appraised the Estate of WILLIAM HARDEN deceased .. items valued and totalled, £ 546.11.9 .. made by appraisers HENRY BREWER, DANIEL SANFORD, JOHN DAVIS ..

At a court held .. 22d Jany 1782 .. inventory returned & ordered to be recorded.

pp. 241-243 DR. Estate of JAMES CONNELL Deceased with the Executors .. (1771) Robt. Adams acct of goods bou't at Vendue, Richard Morris his estate, William Ramsay his account, to Wm. Payne Sheriff, to recording of the will, return of the inventory, recording Estate debt ..

William Ramsay January 18th 1781.

DR. The Estate of JAMES CONNELL in Acct. with the Executors .. (1781) .. cash paid John Sutton ..

Alexandria Febru'ry 27th 1780. Received from William Ramsay £ 7380 also £ 6 15s in lieu of £ 82 1s and 7 pence money that was omitted being the above balance due from the Executors of my late Uncle, JAMES CONNEL Estate settled this day .. JOHN SUTTON.
Witness William Hunter Junr.

JAMES CONNEL Estate Acc'ot. At a court held .. 19th February 1782 .. WILLIAM RAMSAY Executor of JAMES CONNEL Deceased exhibited this account and settlement by JOHN SUTTON heir at law .. is admitted to record.

pp. 243-244 An Inventory of the goods and chattles of the Deceased JOHN WILLIAMSON of Fairfax County being appraised on the Sixth of February 1782 by the Subscribers .. items valued and totalled, £ 36.0.4 .. includes a tomahawk .. made by appraisers BENJAMIN x SUDDETH, JOHN HERYFORD, WM. KEEN ..

At a court held .. 19th Feby 1782 .. inventory returned and ordered to be recorded.

p. 244 Fairfax. June Cort 1781. Ordered that JOHN HERYFORD, WILLIAM HALLY, WILLIAM KEEN and BENJAMIN SUDDETH or any three of them .. appraise the Estate of JOHN WILLIAMSON ..

This day came (those named except William Hally) and was sworn as appraisers to appraise the Estate of JOHN WILLIAMSON Decd. Given 6 day February 1782.

Daniel McCarty

p. 245 Appraisement (no person shown) made January 1782. Aprais'd by ROGER CHEW, EDWARD GAINSAY, JACOB BONBY ..

At a court held .. 19th February 1782 .. inventory returned and ordered to be recorded.

pp. 245-246 January 1782. Return of the Effects Sold from the Estate of JAMES KELLY Deceased .. purchasers .. Colo. Fitzhugh, Mr. Bonce, Mr. Hays Little, Lewis Zimermin, John Williams ..

At a court held .. 19th February 1782 .. Account of Sale returned and ordered to be recorded.

pp. 247-256 Will of JOHN BALENDINE. I JOHN BALENDINE of county of Fairfax at this time of sound disposing Sense .. Executors to take immediate possession of all my Estate on James River and the waters thereof as on Potomack in Virginia and also on Maryland side which said Estate I desire be kept up all together and be carried on for the best advantage .. with regards to my Debts the most of them are from Judgments and Bonds .. judgments obtained by the absence of my attorney on discounts offered in Barr (to wit) ROBERT DOWNMAN ₤ 141 4s and 3 pence .. himself present only complaining of not having credit for an old horse that JOEL WHITE knows was not worth a shilling; LEONARD BALDUS ₤ 69 12s and 3 pence .. given to ELLZEY, FOUSHEE, TABBS Twenty two pounds two shillings no credit for a large quantity of plank as per my Book kept by GEORGE ROSE and his charge against me is wrong that on a first settlement he will have nothing; due BAYLIS'S Executors One hundred and forty pounds and two pence though upon a fair state of our accounts there is a balance in my favour he having omitted a large balance due me in the legacy from BLACKBURNS Estate. ELLZEY has the account and receipt besides there is a very large open account against WILLIAM and JOHN BAYLIS Deceased that they have given no credit for in their account though a just charge per my books and accounts .. I request likewise that EDWARD SNICKERS may be called to a fair settlement he delivered in his account full of erroneous charges and no credit for a mare Twenty two pounds Ten shillings in value in pledge to the Sheriff of Frederick as my bail in the suit of ROBERT RUTHERFORD which they detained and notwithstanding the survey made by Mr. CRAVEN PEYTON of the Overplus land sold he takes no notice upon a just state he will fall in my Debt at least Five hundred and fifty pounds .. With regards to the arbitration with JOHN SIMPLE as far as relates to KEYS land .. and likewise the five thousand acres on the maryland side I do in the most Solemn manner declare my disatesfaction and sincerely intreat to have those two points in dispute settled .. concerning those two disputes the Balance in my favour settled by Mr. ALEXANDER HENDERSON, Mr. HECTOR ROSS .. my desire that the lands at the Seneca Falls where I made Improvements for works and with half the Island in the Bargain reserved from Captain McCARTY in giving up the other part of the Estate as by survey made by said McCARTY which said reservation I desire may be made by Sale for the life of my son, THOMAS WILLIAM BALENDINE. The lands on James River called Etrick Banks purchased of PATRICK COUTTS Esqr. with the Improvements of the canal, Mills, fisheryes, etc., Including Saunders Island are for this year till Christmas rented out to HENRY RIGBY as by agreement lodged in THOMAS BOOTHS hands and the Buckingham Furnace with three thousand acres of land, large stock of Coal and oar and six valuable slaves .. are to be considered free of any encumbrance though the state of Virginia has a mortgage for money furnished yet as they are owing me considerable more for a moiety of their expenses on the canal and dam at Etrick Banks .. Mr. WILLIAM HANSFORD has the management at present if he behaves well and worthy of the good opinion I have always entertained of him it is my advise he should be continued and supported on the same terms Mr. HUNTER gives Mr. VERNON. The three acres of land allotted for the Brewery Company and on which their Brewery stands .. (money not received) .. It is my desire the 26½ acres of land as laid off by Mr. GEORGE WEST county surveyor for which I have a deed from the Late Honourable PHILLIP LUDWELL LEE be improved .. and it being my will that my dear Sister, FRANCES BALENDINE, remove immediately to the falls of the Potomack with all her Slaves, stock, etc. .. and that my son and daughter may be under her Government during the term of the lease .. my desire she be paid annually Ten thousand pounds of crop tobacco and cask during term of said lease and that she may remove to James River or any part of my Estate that she may choose .. debts owing me be got as fast as possible on the judgments I have in Loudoun County against WILLIAM WROE and also that WILLIAM GRAYSON discount Eight pounds Ten for four years service of the Barber for fear it might be forgot, and now having been so particular in my affairs .. my will that my son, THOMAS WILLIAM BALENDINE, should have my Estate .. my will that my daughter, FANNY BALENDINE, be paid the sum of Ten thousand pounds in Specie .. in ten annual payments .. the first on 1st day of January 1785 .. also one acre of land at the falls of the Potomack in the Town of Philee and also one acre of land at the Etrick Banks near the canal on the James river .. to my dear Sister, FRANCES BALENDINE, my gold watch chain .. MR. DOWNMAN a mourning ring .. Mrs. STUBBLEFIELD money sufficient to purchase her a negro girl of twelve or thirteen years .. which I expect she will give to her son, THOMAS, at her death being my Godson .. give said child, THOMAS STUBBLEFIELD, a lot of land in the town of Philee .. to my dear and intimate friend, Mr. RICHARD THOMPSON of George Town in the state of Maryland .. all the lower part of the land I purchased of EDWARD BALL and wife whereon his mill stands .. adjoining lands of COLONEL MURDOCK .. (long discussion of mismanagement of his estate by BLACKBURN & ELLZEY) .. give my three friends each a mourning right as a remembrance of the many happy days passed together on Occoquan .. appoint my dear Sister, FRANCES BALENDINE, and my loving son, THOMAS WILLIAM BALENDINE, Executrix and Executor .. this 3rd day of June 1781 ..

John Balendine

Presence of Evan William, Wm. McDaniel, John Dowing, Charles Attwell

At a court held .. xixth March 1782 .. will presented by THOMAS WILLIAM BALENDINE .. admitted to record .. certificate is granted him for obtaining a probate thereof ..

pp. 256-259 Inventory of Sundry goods belonging to the Estate of Mr. WILLIAM MUNDAY Deceased .. items valued and totalled, Ł 66.6.6 .. given 23rd of May 1782 by appraisers JOHN SAUNDERS, EDWARD RAMSAY, JOHN ELTON. Mentions JOHN SMITH note; to Doctor PLATT TOWNSHEND from PRISSILLA SEBASTIAN ..

At a court held .. 20th August 1782 .. inventory returned and ordered to be recorded.

pp. 259-260 Know all men .. We HENRY GARRETT, HENRY GARRETT JUNR., ED. BLACKBURN are bound unto WM. RAMSAY, ROBERT McCRA, THOMAS LEWIS and HENRY (sic) Gentlemen .. for sum of Two hundred pounds current money of Virginia .. 17th June 1782. Condition .. if HENRY GARRETT and HENRY GARRETT JUNR., guardians of ANN, CHARLES, WILLIAM, DANIEL HARDEN .. do truly pay said Orphion all Estate due them .. obligation to be void ..

Henry Garrett Henry Garrett Junr.
Edward Blackburn

At a court held .. 17th June 1782 .. acknowledged bond which is ordered to be recorded.

pp. 260-262 Will of DANIEL WITHERS COFFER. I DANIEL WITHERS COFFER of Fairfax County being of sound mind and memory .. give all my land unto my son, FRANCIS COFFER .. to my son, JOHN COFFER, a negro girl slave .. to my son, JOSHUA COFFER, a negro girl slave .. to my daughter, SARAH LITTLEJOHN, three slaves already in her possession .. also two other slaves .. to my grandson, THOMAS COFFER, a negro girl slave .. remainder of slaves and other estate .. I give and bequeath to my three sons, FRANCIS, JOHN and JOSHUA, to be equally divided among them .. appoint

my son, FRANCIS, Executor .. this first day January 1781.
Presence Thomas Clarke,
Joseph Ferguson
Thomas Withers Coffer

At a court held .. 16th September 1782 .. will presented by FRANCIS COFFER .. admitted to record .. certificate granted him for obtaining a probate thereof ..

pp. 262-263 Will of ROBERT HARPER. I ROBERT HARPER of Westmoreland County .. give to my loving wife all my Estate .. my estate not be appraised .. appoint my loving wife Executrix .. this 28th day January 1781.
Presence John Washington,
Constant Washington
Robert Harper

At a court held .. 16th September 1782 .. will presented by JOHN WASHINGTON .. JOHN HARPER, SAMUEL EARL and HENRY WASHINGTON made oath will is in the proper hand writing of said Testator which is admitted to record .. certificate granted (JOHN WASHINGTON) for obtaining letters of administration with the will annexed ..

p. 263 I SARAH HARPER widow and relict of ROBERT HARPER late of the county of Fairfax decd do by these presents resign the Executor Ship of the said Harpers will and desire that administration of ROBERT HARPERS Estate may be granted to my Father, JOHN WASHINGTON, Gent. .. this 5th September 1782.
Witness Roger West,
Louisa Washington, Samuel Harper
Sarah Harper

At a court held .. 16th September 1782 .. this resignation was proved .. ordered to be recorded.

p. 264 Inventory of the Estate of ROBERT HARPER Decd .. no value for items or total valuation. JOHN WASHINGTON, admr.

At a court held .. 16th September 1782 .. inventory returned and ordered to be recorded.

pp. 265-267 Will of ROBERT WICKLIFF. I ROBERT WICKLIFF of county of Prince William do make my last will .. devise my lot and house in the Town of Dumfries, my slaves (4 named) and all the residue of my Estate to my wife, MARY WICKLIFF, during her life and after her decease I give the same to such child, children and grandchildren as she may have living at the time of her death .. if she has no child or grandchildren at her death, I give to my Brother, CHARLES WICKLIFF, LYDIA his wife .. I give my waring cloaths to ARRINGTON WICKLIFF. I desire ELIAS WICKLIFF may be schooled three years out of my Estate whose board is also to be provided .. appoint my wife, MARY WICKLIFF, & my Brother, CHARLES WICKLIFF, Executrix & Executor .. this 25th day April 1773.
Presence Cuth. Bullitt,
Thos. Dagg, Elizabeth x Murdock
Rob. Wickliff

Codicil dated 30th April 1773 .. clarifies bequest to wife ..

At a court held .. 16th September 1782 .. will presented by MARY WICKLIFF and CHARLES WICKLIFF .. admitted to record .. certificate granted them for obtaining a probate thereof ..

pp. 267-269 Will of ELIZABETH BUCHANAN. I ELIZABETH BUCHANAN late of Annarundale County in State of Maryland now of Alexandria County of Fairfax & State of Virginia being weak and infirm in body .. give and bequeath and devise to MARGARET, the wife of JOHN GRETTER, of the aforesaid Town of Alexandria all my Estate .. at her death the same to devolve to BETTY and JOHN, the daughter and son of MARGARET and JOHN GRATTER to be equally divided between them .. appoint MARGARET GRETTER and none other sole Executor .. this 13th day July 1782.

Presence Wm. Hepburn, Jno. Short, Charles Bryan — Eliz. Buchanan

At a court held .. 16th September 1782 .. will presented by MARGARET GRETTER .. admitted to record .. certificate granted her for obtaining a probate thereof ..

pp. 269-270 An Inventory and appraisement of such of the personal Estate of ROBERT BAYLEY deceased as was presented to our view by SAMUEL BAYLEY administrator this 14th day of August 1782 .. items valued and totalled, ₤ 20.11.7½ .. made by appraisers CLEON MOORE, JOHN HEDGMAN, EDWARD WASHINGTON JUNR. .. Court order appointing appraisers (including JOHN GIBSON) follows inventory.

At a court held .. 17th September 1782 .. inventory returned and ordered to be recorded.

pp. 271-274 DR. (1772) Estate of EDWARD RIGDEN to THOS. RIGDEN .. a legacy due me by my fathers estate; Thomas Davis's account; Michel Gretter, John Clifford's account against the Estate of my Father for Partridge; Doctr. Brown's account; Michel Martin's account; Andrew Wales account; Roger Chew's account for appraisement; Willm. Shaw's account; Peter Robinsons account; Thomas Flemings account; Charles Jones pasture; Mr. Richd. Arrel, Elizabeth Rigdens purchase at sale; James Kirk, William Carlins account; John Bowling; Cyrus Copper, Wm. Barker, Pearce Bailey; Thos. Brownly; Richard Lake; Estate of JAMES CONNEL; Wm. Munday for Doctr. Townshend; John Dalton; Richard Harrison by Robt. Adam; Wm. Bushbys account; balance due JAMES CONNELL. Contra. Judgment against Geo. Alexander ..

At a court held .. 17th September 1782 .. THOMAS RIGDEN admr. of EDWARD RIGDEN exhibited this account .. is allowed and ordered to be recorded.

pp. 274-288 An Inventory and appraisement of the Estate of JOHN PARK CUSTIS Esqr. deceased taken the 20th day February 1782 for the county of Fairfax .. items valued and totalled, ₤ 2977.5.6 and ₤ 3582 for 73 slaves named and appraised for total inventory amount of ₤ 6559.5.6 .. large number of books listed .. made by appraisers GEORGE GILPIN, WM. HERBERT, CHARLES LITTLE. February Court 1782 appraisers appointed and also included THOMAS HERBERT .. sworn before ROBERT ADAM ..

At a court held .. 18th September 1782 .. inventory returned and ordered to be recorded.

pp. 288-291 An appraisement of the Estate of ELIZABETH BUCHANAN Deceased .. items valued and totalled, ₤ 102.2.6 .. made by appraisers LAWRANCE HOOFF, RALPH LONGDON, JAMES PARSONS, CHARLES BRYAN .. September Court 1782 appraisers appointed .. sworn before WM. RAMSAY ..

At a court held .. 21st October 1782 .. inventory returned and ordered to be recorded.

pp. 292-295 Will of GEORGE SIMPSON. This Fourteenth day of October 1782 I GEORGE SIMPSON of county of Fairfax being very sick and weak in body .. give and bequeath to my Loving wife, SUSANNA SIMPSON, during her life the plantation I now live on which formerly was bought of JOHN PARSONS with the use of four slaves (Vizt. Catral, Bess that is now living at home Jeremiah, Jabbock) .. (other animals, furniture and utensils) .. after her decease my son, RICHARD SIMPSON, to come in for the land. I give my son, WILLIAM SIMPSON, 100 acres of land where he now lives. I give my son, AARON SIMPSON, the remainder of that Track. I give to my son, GEORGE SIMPSON, and my son, JAMES SIMPSON, 256 acres whereon I formerly lived lying on the Ox Road .. JAMES SIMPSON to have the upper end whereon LANCELOT BECK now lives. I give to my son, JOSEPH SIMPSON, that track of land known by the name of Hambletons. I give to my son, RICHARD SIMPSON, one slave and one orpen boy named JOHN DILLEN. I give to my son, WILLIAM SIMPSON, one slave named Wolf Run Bess and her increase. I give to my son, AARON SIMPSON, one slave .. to my son, GEORGE SIMPSON, one slave .. to my son, JAMES SIMPSON, two slaves .. to my son, JOSEPH, one slave. I give my Daughter, MARY SIMPSON, one slave .. and for my daughter who has married off and left me I have given them their equal part .. my plantation on Wolf Run I leave to be sold .. appoint my Brother, MOSES SIMPSON, RICHARD SIMPSON my son and AARON SIMPSON Executors ..

Teste Richd. Wheeler, George Simpson
John Simpson, Benj. x Suddeth
James Aldridge

Codicil gives corn and wheat to wife, the small still, the apple mill and all my casks ..

At a court held .. 18th November 1782 .. will presented by MOSES SIMPSON and AARON SIMPSON .. admitted to record .. certificate is granted them for obtaining a probate thereof ..

pp. 295-298 Will of GEORGE ROBERTSON. The twenty third day of September 1782 I GEORGE ROBERSON of county of Fairfax being very sick .. my estate is to be equally divided between my son, JAMES ROBERTSON, my daughter, SUSANNA ROBERTSON, and my son, WILLIAM ROBERTSON. My desire my three children may have sufficient schooling .. my desire Mr. GEORGE SIMPSON SNR. bring up my children .. if he dies his son, WILLIAM SIMPSON, may have the care of them. Constitute WILLIAM SIMPSON, AARON SIMPSON and RICHARD WHEELAR Executors ..

Presence William x Simpson, George Robertson
Joseph x Blancet, Thos. Gossom

At a court held .. 18th November 1782 .. will presented by WILLIAM SIMPSON .. admitted to record .. certificate granted him for obtaining a probate thereof ..

pp. 298-301 Will of EDWARD DULIN. I EDWARD DULIN of Fairfax parrash in county of Fairfax being in perfect health .. doe this 12th day February 1778 make my last will and testament. I give and bequeath to my well beloved son, WILLIAM DULIN, the tract of land on which he now lives with half the stock that is on the plantation .. also one negro man & one negro boy .. for want of heirs to be equally divided amongst the rest of my children. I give to my Daughter, ELIZABETH SUMMERS, one negro lad .. also one negro girl. I give to my Daughter, ANNE DULIN, one negro lad also one boy. I give my Daughter, SALLY DULIN, one negro lad also one negro girl. I give my son, EDWARD DULIN, one negro woman one child also one negro boy. I give to my well beloved son, JOHN DULIN, one negro woman, one negro boy & one boy .. to my son, EDWARD DULING, and my son, JOHN DULING, to be equally divided the tract of land that I now live on .. also the money that is due me from Capt. WILLIAM DOUGLASS when collected .. Seventy five pounds each to give

them schooling .. remainder to my well beloved wife, SARAH DULIN .. after her death to be equally divided among all my Legatees .. appoint my well beloved wife, SARAH DULIN, & my son, WILLIAM DULIN, & my son in law, JOHN SUMMERS, to be my Executors ..
Presence Jeremiah Williams, Ed. Dulin
James Cockerill, Jain Williams,
William Tasker

At a court held .. 18th November 1782 .. will presented by SARAH DULIN, WILLIAM DULIN and JOHN SUMMERS .. admitted to record .. certificate is granted them for obtaining a probate thereof ..

pp. 301-302 Will of BENJAMIN COLELOUGH. I BENJAMIN COLELOUGH of Warren County north carolina State being low in health .. give and bequeath unto my Brother, WRUE COLELOUGH, the lot that belongs in Warrenton No. 97 .. if the law permitted any time hereafter to have my negro wench named Wrose and her child and the heirs of her body hereafter born to be set free as they come to age twenty one .. Cousen, JANNY, the knives cost about two dollars & one sixteenth but for fear of your lying out of it to Long I allow you Three Dollars ..
Witness Drakeford Gray, Benja. Colelough
Presley Gay

At a court held .. 21st October 1782 .. will presented by DRAKEFORD GRAY .. admitted to record .. certificate granted him for obtaining letters of administration with will annexed ..

pp. 302-303 We the Subscribers have appraised the Estate of BENJA. COLELOUGH Decd as far as was presented to our view & have Inventory'd the same .. items valued and totalled, £ 42.3.10 .. made by appraisers RICHARD RATCLIFF, WILLIAM STONE, JOHN COTTON ..

At a court held .. 18th November 1782 .. inventory returned and ordered to be recorded.

p. 303 1782. DR. Estate of BENJA. COLELOUGH Decd to DRD. GRAY .. nine days attendance on you when down with small pox; supplying you with a woman to nurse you; shirt and sundry grave cloths; paid Richard Ratcliff for selling Estate ..

At a court held .. 18th November 1782 .. DRAKEFORD GRAY admr. of BENJAMIN COLELOUGH deceased exhibited this account .. is allowed and ordered to be recorded.

pp. 304-305 Know all men .. we SARAH DULIN, WILLIAM DULIN & JEREMIAH WILLIAMS are bound unto DANIEL McCARTY, WILLIAM RAMSAY, ROBERT T. HOOE, ROBERT McCREA, THOS. LEWIS & JOHN GIBSON, Gentlemen Justices of the county court of Fairfax .. in sum of Four thousand pounds current money of Virginia .. 19th November 1782. Condition .. if SARAH DULIN, Guardian of EDWARD and JOHN DULIN .. shall pay all estate .. due said orphans .. obligation to be void ..

Sarah x Dulin
William x Dulin
Jeremiah Williams

At a court held .. 19th November 1782 .. acknowledged bond which was ordered to be recorded.

pp. 305-306 Know all men .. We CHARLES HARDEN & MOSES BALL are bound unto DANIEL McCARTY, ROBERT T. HOOE, WM. RAMSAY & ROB. McCRAE Gentlemen Justices of the county court of Fairfax .. in the sum of Two thousand pounds current money of Virginia .. 19th November 1782. Condition ..

if CHARLES HARDEN Guardian of THOMAS GREEN HARDEN .. shall pay all estate due said orphan .. obligation to be void ..

At a court held .. 19th November 1782 .. bond acknowledged and ordered to be recorded.
Charles Harden
Moses Ball

pp. 306-312 We the Subscribers have Inventoryed and appraised all the Estate of JOHN HEATON Deceased that was presented to our view .. items valued and totalled, £ 295.7.7 .. made by appraisers JOHN GIBSON, JOHN MILLS, WM. BAYLY .. who were sworn before A. HENDERSON ..

At a court held .. 18th February 1783 .. inventory returned and ordered to be recorded.

pp. 312-325 Sale of goods belonging to the Estate of JOHN HEATON Deceas'd at Colchester by Publick Vendue the 17th & 18th days of June 1784 (sic) to whom sold .. Thos. Church, Wm. McDaniel, Andrew Garden, Thos. Songster, Alexander Henderson, John Gibson, Terner Crump, George Calvert, Daniel McCarty, William Bayly, Sampson Turley, John Tillet, Andrew Gordon, Spence Grayson, Robert Church, Wm. Stone, Thomas Windsor, William Thompson, George Lewis, James Lawson, Dr. James Nesbitt, George Purvis, James Moore, Hardage Lane, Geo. Lamkin, William Hartshorne, Jno. Gunnell, Vincent Cooksy, William Coarts, William Lindsay, William McAtee, Edward Washington Senr., Thomas Simmons, John Rearden, Peeter Coulter, Daniel Rurick, Major Wagener, James Hardage Lane, Charles Carnish, Lewis Hipkins, Thomas Lucas, Shadrick Green, Thomas Hornbuckle, Francis Stone, Moses Simpson, William Edwards, Sarah Athey, Edward Washington Junr., John Mills, Peter Wagener .. total value of sale £ 267.17. 9 3/4 ..

At a court held .. 18th February 1783 .. This account of sales was returned and ordered to be recorded.

pp. 326-328 Will of SOPHIA BEALL. I SOPHIA BEALL of the Brough of Alexandria and Fairfax County, widow, being sick .. give and bequeath to my dearly beloved granddaughter, ELIZABETH MOXLY, my negro woman .. remaining part of my estate to be sold at publick auction .. money I give and bequeath to my three daughters, CHARITY MAGRUDER, HESTER MOXLY, CASSIA WHITE .. appoint my son in law, THOMAS MOXLY, sole Executor .. this 8th day of May 1782.

Presence of George Row, Phillop Webster, John x Lott
Sophia Beall

At a court held .. 18th February 1783 .. will presented by THOMAS MOXLEY .. admitted to record .. certificate granted for obtaining a probate thereof ..

pp. 328-334 We have valued and appraised the Estate of EDWARD DULIN Deceast as was presented to our view .. items valued and totalled, £ 1300.2.7½ .. made by appraisers JOHN DULIN, ELIE STONE, GEO. MINOR ..

At a court held .. 17th March 1783 .. ordered to be recorded.

pp. 334-335 We the Subscribers have Divided and set apart the Estate of WILLIAM HARDEN Decd between the said Decedents Widdow and his son, THOMAS GREEN HARDEN. Division presented in two columns but no value assigned items .. made by WILLIAM ADAMS, JAMES HURST, ALLEN DAVIS ..

At a court held .. 19th March 1784 .. ordered to be recorded.

pp. 335-336 We RICHARD WHEELAR, JOSEPH BENNET and GEORGE NICKELS are bound unto DANIEL McCARTY, CHAS. BROADWATER, ROBERT McCREA, ROB. T. HOOE & JOHN GIBSON Gentlemen Justices of the county court of Fairfax .. in the sum of Seven hundred pounds current money of Virginia .. 17th March 1783. Condition if RICHARD WHEELAR Guardian of JOHN SIMPSON ..

shall pay all estate due said orphan .. obligation to be void ..
At a court held .. 17th March 1783 .. acknowledged bond which is ordered to be recorded.
Richard Wheelar
Joseph Bennett
George Nickalls

pp. 337-338 An inventory of the goods and effects of JOHN SHAW deceased .. items valued and totalled, ₤ 21.19.6. Alexandria March 11, 1783, we JOHN LOMAX, WILLIAM WARD, PHILLIP WEBSTER & JOHN LONGDON .. have appraised the estate of JOHN SHAW Deceased and returned this as a true inventory of same ..
At a court held .. 17th 1783 (sic) .. inventory returned and ordered to be recorded.

pp. 338-339 March 13th 1783. An Inventory of a parcel of goods belonging to SOFYEARS BEAL deceased valued by ROGER CHEW, JOHN LONGDON & WILLIAM WARD .. items valued and totalled, ₤ 22.6.4 ..
At a court held .. 17th 1783 (sic) .. inventory returned and ordered to be recorded.

pp. 339-342 An appraisement of the personal estate of WILLIAM SHAW Deceased taken by us the Subscribers appointed by the Court for the said purpose July 28th 1775 (sic) .. items valued and totalled, ₤ 202.12.6 .. made by appraisers JAMES CONNELL, ROBERT McCREA, JAMES HENDERSON ..
At a court held .. 18th March 1783 .. inventory returned and ordered to be recorded.

pp. 342-345 Sails of the Estate of WILLIAM SHAW Deceased by ROBERT McCREA & ELENOR SHAW, Executors, sold at 12 months credit .. Mathew Campbell Servt. man Peter Holims, Richard Stewart and Henry Hall; books to Thos. Kirk, Charles Turner, Robert Adam, Mathew Campbell, Andrew Wells, John Brooks; other items sold to Windsor Brown, Thomas Moxley, Thomas Kirkpatrick, Charles Broadwater Junr., John Orr, Alexander Chisholm, Andrew Wells, John Grayham, John Harper, Doctr. Wm. Brown, Andrew Wales, John Loman, John Shaw, Robert Lindsay ..
At a court held .. 18th March 1783 .. This acct of Sails returned and ordered to be recorded.

pp. 345-348 Inventory of sundry goods belonging to JAMES MURE deceased made by WILLIAM HERBERT, MR. JOHN MURE & Mr. ROBERT McCREA .. Alexandria 10th October 1780. Items valued and totalled, ₤ 3275.2.0 ..
At a court held .. 18th March 1783 .. inventory returned and ordered to be recorded.

pp. 348-350 List of sundries sold at Vendue Octr. 18th 1780 for Mr. ADAMS .. amount given in dollars (total 13,960) and pounds (total 5,661) .. (a continuation of the sale of the Estate of JAMES MUIR) ..
At a court held .. 18th March 1783 .. account of Sails returned and ordered to be recorded.

pp. 350-351 March Court 1783. Ordered that ADAM LYNN, RALPH LONGDON, WILLIAM DUVALL and ROGER CHEW or any three .. appraise all the Estate of FREDRICK HENENGER deceased which shall be presented to their vew and and that the administratrix return same to next court. Sworn before JAMES HENDRICKS 26th Apl. 1783. Items valued and totalled, ₤ 53.19.6.
At a court held .. 19th May 1783 .. inventory returned and ordered to be recorded.

p. We the Subscribers have sold to the highest bidder all the personal
352 estate of DAVID YOUNG Deceased that was produced to us by Mr. RALPH LONGDON in order to make an equal division among the said decedents children .. The sale totalled £ 48.16.0. Deduct charges for drumer, 4/6; for cryer, 1.4.0; for rum, 0.10.0 .. divided among four, £ 46.17.6 .. each child a proportion of £ 11.14.3. Mr. VALENTINE UHLER has received for the Eldest; Mr. RALPH LONGDON for the second and for the other two the Court will please to give directions. Alexandria 20th August 1782 .. ADAM LYNN, W. McKNIGHT, JAMES PARSONS.

At a court held .. 20th May 1783 .. Division of Estate returned and ordered to be recorded.

pp. Fairfax Septemr. Court 1782. Ordered WILLIAM REARDEN, JOHN FOWLAR,
352- JOHN RAGAN and HENRY BOGGESS or any three of them .. Inventory and
354 appraise all the Estate of JOSIAS PAYNE deceased which shall be presented to their view and that the administratrix return same to next Court .. Sworn (except Henry Boggess) 12th December 1782 before DANIEL McCARTY. Items valued and totalled, £ 303.13.6 ..

At a court held .. 19th May 1783 .. inventory returned and ordered to be recorded.

pp. DR. Estate of JOHN HEATON in Acct with WILLIAM HARTSHORN .. expense
355- to Colchester and for punch at the vendue; to Andrew Gordon; paid
360 Richard Lee for bond; Robert Harrison a fee for his advice; paid tax for four wheeled carriage; paid for goods bot of JAMES McDANIEL at Richmond October 1770 .. Jno. Gunnell for crying in June 1774 .. Contra. 1774-1778. James Nesbit, John Mills, James Lawson, Wm. Cullison, Peter Coulter, Thos. Harbuckle, Wm. McAtee, John Tillet, Thos. Church, Moses Simpson, Andw. Gordon, William Courts, James Doneal, Thos. Songster, Jno. Aitchison, Wm. McDaniel, Jno. Harper, Angel Jordon, James Hardage Lane, Edward Washington, James Edwards, Wm. Stone, James Moore, Sarah Athy, John Gibson, Alexander Henderson, Michel Thorn, Daniel McArty, Geo. Lewis, George Purvis, Henry Moore, Spence Grayson, John Gunnell, Gilbert Rowland, Geo. Lamkin, Sampson Turley, Lewis Hipkins .. Alexandria February 18th 1783.

At a court held .. 17th June 1783 .. WILLIAM HARTSHORN administrator of the Estate of JOHN HEATON deceased exhibited this account .. is allowand and admitted to record.

pp. Fairfax May Court 1783. Ordered that GEORGE SMITH, WILLIAM WREN,
360- THADDEUS DULIN & CHARLES THRIFT or any three .. Inventory & appraise
361 all the estate of WILLIAM SHORTRIDGE decd which shall be presented to their view and the admor. return same to next Court .. appraised estate 14th June 1783 .. items valued and totalled, £ 10.11.0 .. made by appraisers GEORGE SMITH, WM. WREN, THADDEUS DULIN.

At a court held .. 16th June 1783 .. inventory returned and ordered to be recorded.

pp. We the Subscribers have appraised the Estate of GEORGE ROBERTSON
361- Deceased that was presented to our view by WILLIAM SIMPSON Executor
363 .. items valued and totalled, £ 237.11.4 .. appraisal November 30th 1782 by EDWARD FORD, JOHN TILLETT, JOHN SIMPSON ..

At a court held .. 17th June 1783 .. inventory returned and ordered to be recorded.

pp. An Inventory of the Sale of the goods and chattles of the deceased
363- GEORGE ROBERTSON 1782 .. shows items sold and amount paid but no pur-
365 chasers .. total amount of the sale, £ 200.5.1 ..

At a court held .. 17th June 1783. This Sale of the Estate of GEORGE ROBERTSON Decd was returned and ordered to be recorded.

pp. Fairfax September Court 1783. Ordered that FRANCIS WARMAN, WILLIAM
366- NORRIS, JOHN SCOTT & PHILLOP ATKINS or any three .. Inventory and ap-
367 praise all the Estate of ROBERT WICKLIFF Deceased in the county of Mohongohaly which shall be presented to their view and that the Executors return the same to next Court ..

Mohongohaly County 18th October 1782. WILLIAM NORRIS, JOHN SCOTT & PHILLOP ATKINS .. qualified .. Sworn before F. NORMAN.

We the Subscribers hath made a true Perfect Inventory of the Estate of ROBT. WICKLIFF Deceased Vizt. Octr. 18th 1782 .. items valued and totalled, £ 94.10.6 ..

At a court held .. 19th Augt. 1783 .. inventory returned and ordered to be recorded.

pp. Inventory of Colo. JOHN CARLYLES Estate Real & Personal taken
368- 13th Novemr. 1780 .. among numerous items .. 2 Old trumpets and 1
394 French horn; 1 picture of Bates & 3 tomahawks; 1 scarlet Cloth jacket with broad gold lace; 1 Crimson Velvet do; 1 brown Damask jacket; 1 pr black velvet breaches; 1 pr Crimson knitt & 1 black breaches; 1 scarlet Breaches with gold knee bands; 2 prs Silver shoe Buckles & 1 pr gold studds; 1 Silver free mason medal square, one parcel of old gold and silver lace some melted; 2 gold mourning rings; 1 small free mason gold medal; 1 lead snuff box & tooth pick case; 4 prs Spectacles with cases; 1 backgammon table; 1 Box with four wiggs & 1 old umbrella; 9 slaves listed by name; books; 15 more slaves listed by name .. each item valued and totalled, £ 792.10.5 ..

Inventory of the Estate belonging to Colo. JNO. CARLYLE at Tarthorwald .. mostly cattle, plantation utensils and tools and 43 slaves listed by name .. each item valued and totalled, £ 717.16.8½ ..

At a court held .. 19th August 1783 .. inventory returned and ordered to be recorded.

pp. Fairfax November Court 1782. Ordered that CHARLES LITTLE, CHARLES
394- (sic), THOMAS HERBERT and RICHARD SANFORD JUNR., or any three .. in-
397 ventory and appraise the Estate of PRESLEY COX deceased which shall be presented to their view and that the admr. return the same to next Court .. CHARLES LITTLE, CHARLES JONES & THOS. HERBERT .. sworn before GEORGE GILPIN, Decr. 17th 1782.

An Inventory of the Estate of PRESLY COX Deceased this 18th day December 1782 .. items valued and totalled, £ 176.17.0 .. presented 10th day September 1783.

At a court held .. 15th Setmr. 1783 .. inventory returned and ordered to be recorded.

pp. We the Subscribers have appraised the Estate of IGNATIOUS BAGGETT
397- Decd in the county aforesaid (Fairfax) an inventory of which is as
399 follows 11th November 1783 .. items valued and totalled, £ 29.2.6 .. made by appraisers RICHARD SANFORD, MICHAL AHFORD, RICHARD SANFORD JUNR. ..

At a court held .. 15th Septmr. 1783 .. inventory returned and ordered to be recorded.

pp. 399-400 Know all men .. We SUSANNA PATTERSON, WM. PATTERSON, THOS. PATTERSON & ROBT. BOGGESS are bound unto GEO. MASON, D. McCARTY, WM. RAMSAY, ALEX. HENDERSON & HENRY DARNE Gent. Justices of the county court of Fairfax .. in the sum of One thousand pounds currrent money of Virginia .. 20th October 1783. Condition .. if bound SUSANNAH PATTERSON of BETTY PATTERSON (sic) .. shall truly pay said orphan all estate that will come to (her) hands .. obligation to be void ..

Presence of Pet. Wagener — Susanah Patterson, W. Patterson, Thos. Patterson, Robert Boggess

At a court held .. xxth October 1783 .. acknowledged bond which is ordered to be recorded.

pp. 400-407 Fairfax August Court 1782. Ordered that JOHN TURLEY, JOILES TURLEY, LEWIN GIBBS and GEORGE GIBBS or any three .. appraise all the Estate of WILLIAM PAYNE decd which shall be presented to their view in London (sic) County & that the Executors return the same to the next Court.

Loudoun County. We the Subscribers have Inventory'd and appraised all the Estate of WILLIAM PAYNE Decd in the said County of Loudoun which is presented to us .. lists one old book and 1 negro wench .. given 12th day Septr. 1782 by appraisers JAS. LEWIN GIBBS, JOHN TURLEY, GILES TURLEY .. sworn before PEIRCE BAYLY.

Inventory of goods & chattles of WILLIAM PAYNE Decd taken this 21st day of August 1782 by JOHN DULIN, EDWARD DULIN & DANIAL MILLS, Praisers .. items valued and totalled, Ł 987.12.7 .. We the Subscribers .. also certify that Mr. ED. DULIN Decd was present at the appraisement of the above inventory as an appraiser agreed to the above .. JOHN DULIN, DANELL MILLS.

Inventory of WM. PAYNE Decd Estate & appraisement .. lists one negro with appraised value of Ł 45 .. made by appraisers CHAS. BROADWATER, JOHN DULIN, DANIEL MILLS.

At a court held .. 16th Septr. 1783 .. inventory returned and ordered to be recorded.

pp. 407-409 Will of GRACIE BROWN. I GRACIE BROWN relict of WILLIAM BROWN late of Fairfax County being sick and weak .. do devise and bequeath unto WILLIAM HUNTER JUNR. Esqr. Merchant in Alexandria all my Estate .. and do hereby appoint said WILLIAM HUNTER JUNIOR sole Executor .. this 18th day October 1783 ..

Presence James x Downs, William x Downs, Jno. Oliphant — Grace x Brown

At a court held .. 17th Novemr. 1783 .. will presented .. admitted to record .. certificate is granted him in behalf of COLIN DUNLAP Son & Co. for obtaining administration with the will annexed ..

pp. 409-412 DR. The Estate of HARRISON MANLEY decd to THOS. TRIPLETT decd .. paid Mr. Hector Ross bond; paid Doctor Rumneys account; paid George Gilpin for 9¼ yards White Jeans to line the coffin; paid Thomas Pollard Churchwarden bond for a pew in Pohick Church; parson Dade for sermon; Mrs. Sarah Manleys account; Mrs. Margaret Manley from Col. Washington a wheat account, also to her for inoculation; Robert Boggess acct; John McKensey for smiths work; Rob. Douglass for crying sale; Thos. Baggett for Tob. Hogshead; Mr. Donaldson for schooling 3 children; Wm. Kay for weaving; Mr. Edwd. Sanford to supply the children with necessaries; cash to Mr. Sanford to purchase a gown for SALLY MANLEY; Thomas Triplett commission. Contra. Mr. John Thorntons bond; recd of Col. Washington to purchase Morning etc., James Richards; Thos. Pollard; MARGT. MANLEYS part of SARAH MANLEYS acct agst ye Estate; Mr. Lund Washington account; from James Wrens Executor; John Hammet due on bond; Jacob Cox; James Parsons, Richard Taylor (each for hire of a slave); Craven Peyton acct. .. SARAH TRIPLETT administratrix of THOS. TRIPLETT Decd ..

At a court held .. 15th Septmbr. 1783 .. SARAH TRIPLETT Administratrix of THOMAS TRIPLETT deceased who was Executor of the last will and testament of HARRISON MANLEY deceased exhibited this account .. against said Manleys Estate .. is allowed and ordered to be recorded.

pp. 413-415 Will of CHRISTIAN LANGMARCH. I CHRISTIAN LANGMARCH of Town of Alexandria being weak in body .. give bequeath and divise all that belongs or appertains to me in the United States of America unto my friend, OLIVER PRICE, of Town of Alexandria .. part of a lott or half acre of land in Town of Alexandria and numbered 48, the said part conveyed by Indenture bearing date the 16th day of June 1773 from RICHARD AREL and ELONER his wife to ANGLE HART COUTER subjected to an annual rent of Twenty five dollars .. appointing him said OLIVER PRICE my sole Executor .. this 17th day September 1783.

Presence Edwd. Sanford, James Patton, John Dagg — Christian Langmarch

At a court held .. 16th Decmr. 1783 .. will presented by OLIVER PRICE .. admitted to record .. certificate is granted him for obtaining a probate thereof ..

pp. 415-416 Will of JOHN BLATT. During the illness of Mr. JOHN BLATT, I sat up with him one night alone at Mr. JOHN FITZGERALDS in the course of which night he appear'd to me to be extremely ill but perfectly in his senses he told me he conceived himself to be in great danger & thought it would be necessary for to mention in what manner he would wish to have his property disposed of in case of an accident of that kind which he much apprehended the following was what he wished to be done Vizt. In the first place he requested that all the propity belonging to him in the hands of Mr. HENRY ROSS whom he informed me was his Uncle might be kept by him to the use of himself & his Heirs forever. Secondly he desired that all the money due him in this Town might be collected & after paying his just debts therefrom the Ballance he requested might be applied to the Education of Mr. JOHN FOWLARS son, WILLIAM FOWLAR, whom he informed me was his Godson. Thirdly he requested that Mr. CHARLES URQUART might have all his cloths Except his Linnen and Stockings which he requested my Exceptance of ..

Robert Brent

Fairfax County to wit:

ROBERT BRENT made oath to the truth of the facts stated in the above writing before JOSIAH WATSON, 6th Decr. 1783.

pp. 416-417 Will of CORDELIA DORRELL. I CORDELIA DORRELL of Fairfax County being in perfect mind .. give and bequeath to my dear & well beloved Mother, MARY DORRELL, one negro woman .. after her decease to fall to my dear & well beloved Sister, ANNE BROOKE .. unto my dear & well beloved Sister, ELIZABETH DORRELL, two negroes .. unto WALTER DORRALL BROOKE, son of WALTER BROOKE & ANNE BROOK his wife one negro boy .. unto my dear & well beloved Brother, PHILOP DORRELL, one bay horse ..

unto my dear & well beloved neace, MARY SMITH DORRELL, daughter of PHILLOP DORRELL & SARAH DORRALL, his wife, one negro child .. my will that WILLIAM DORRELL and WALTER BROOKE be Executors .. this 17th day July 1782.

Presence Henry S. Lane, Cordelia Dorrell
Sampson Dorrell

At a court held .. 16th Septr. 1782 .. will proved by HENRY SMITH LANE & SAMPSON DORRELL and admitted to record.

pp. 417-418 Will of GASPER BALSOR. This second day of April 1782, I GASPER BALSOR being very sick & weak in body .. give and bequeath to my grandson, JOHN FIELDS, six pounds hard money to be paid when he comes of age .. to my two younger daughters, CATHARINE and ELIZABETH, all the remainder of my estate .. appoint my loving friend, MICHAL DOWNEY and CHRISTOPHER SLIMMER, my executors .. my desire & positive orders that my Executors have the bringing up and sole care of my two children ..

Presence William Biehead (?), Gasper x Balsor
Pearson Thrift, Thomas Ramsay

At a court held .. 16th April 1782 .. will presented (by Executors) .. admitted to record .. certificate granted them for obtaining a probate thereof ..

pp. 419-422 We the subscribers JOHN HARPER, WASHER BLUNT, JOSEPH COVERLY and JAMES LAWRASON being appointed to inventory and appraise all the estate of doctor BENJAMIN CHAPPIN deceased the goods and chattles to us presented .. items valued and totalled, £ 183.12.10 .. sworn 13th April 1782 before JAMES HENDRICKS ..

At a court held .. 16th April 1782 .. inventory returned and ordered to be recorded.

pp. 422-423 Will of WILLIAM MUNDAY. I WILLIAM MUNDAY of Town of Alexandria County of Fairfax being enferm in body .. give and bequeath to my beloved wife, ELIZABETH, all my household furniture, my tools of occupation, Books of all kinds, Notes of hand Book debts to be disposed of at her discrition likewise the interest of certificate amounting to two thousand dollars so long as the principal remains unpaid .. also a lott I possess on ground rent in the lotts adjoining the Town of Alexandria numbered 150 .. the Two thousand dollars in certificates when paid to purpose of satisfying Doctr. PLATT TOWNSHEND for the many favours I have receaved at his hands .. appoint LEWIS WESTON & SAML. ARELL Executors .. March 2d 1782.

Witness George Mason, William Munday
John x Horn, John Smith

At a court held .. xxth May 1782 .. will presented by LEWIS WESTON .. admitted to record .. certificate is granted him for obtaining a probate thereof ..

pp. 424-425 Will of WILLIAM RUMNEY. The nuncupative will of WILLIAM RUMNEY doctor of Physick spoken and declared in our presents the thirteenth day of December last he being at that time of sound mind and memory Vizt. He directed that his negro man London should be perfectly free that Mr. ROBERT ADAM should have the sole direction and management of his affairs and gave to the said ROBERT all his Estate except his negro man London. He particularised a debt that was owing to him from the Estate of JOHN PARK CUSTUS of Two hundred pounds including the inoculation of seventy or eighty slaves, also a debt due to him from the Estate of THOMAS ADDISON of at least Two hundred pounds. The said WILLIAM RUMNEY departed this life the Eighth day of this Instant and on the Ninth day January 1783 we have reduced this nuncupative will to writing.

David Stuart W. Brown
Thos. Kirkpatrick Peter Dow

At a court held .. 18th Feby 1783 .. will presented by ROBERT ADAM Gent. .. admitted to record .. certificate granted him for obtaining a probate thereof ..

pp. 425-427 April 29th 1782. We the Subscribers have Inventoryed and appraised all the Estate of GASPER BOLSER decd that was presented to our view in hard cash .. items valued and totalled, ₤ 65.11.0 .. made by appraisers JOHN KEYTH, JAS. WREN, WM. GUNNELL SNR.

At a court held .. xxth May 1782 .. ordered to be recorded.

pp. 427-428 Know all men .. We PEIRCE BAYLY & PETER WAGENER are bound unto GEO. GILPIN, ROBERT McCREA, JAS. HENDRICKS & CHAS. LITTLE Gentlemen Justices of the county court of Fairfax .. in the sum of Six hundred pounds current money of Virginia .. 20th August 1782. Condition .. if PEIRCE BAYLY guardian of DEVALL PAYNE .. shall pay said orphan all such estate as soon as orphan shall attain to lawful age .. obligation to be void ..

At a court held .. 20th August 1782 .. Peirce Bayly Pet. Wagener acknowledged bond which was ordered to be recorded.

pp. 428-439 We WILLIAM HUNTER, COLEN McIVER and SAML. ARELL being appointed to appraise the Effects of JAMES STEWART Decd do Inventory and appraise the same .. items valued and totalled, ₤ 451.16.5¼ .. sworn before CHARLES LITTLE May 21st 1782 ..

At a court held .. 17th June 1782 .. ordered to be recorded.

pp. 439-441 Will of WILLIAM BAYLY. I WILLIAM BAYLY of Colchester in county of Fairfax being of sound and perfect mind .. and whereas given and made my sons, PIERCE BAYLY, WILLIAM BAYLY, MOUNTJOY BAYLY deeds for their proportion of my Estate I think it needless to mention them. I give my son, SAMUEL BAYLY, the tract of land about 200 acres part of a tract of land I purchased of JOHN EDMONDSON lying under the blue ridge joining the land my son, PIERCE BAYLY, sold also the land my son, MOUNTJOY, sold to DEMSY CARROLL but if he dies without heirs .. my desire JOSEPH BAYLY should enjoy it and for want of such heirs to my son, TAPLEY. I give to my son, JOSEPH BAYLY, and my son, TAPLEY BAYLY, all the remainder of my land under the Blue ridge, JOSEPH BAYLY to have the part my Quarter was on and TAPLY BAYLY the part that Boggess is on joining FRANCIS ERONEMUS .. give to my son, ROBERT BAYLY, all this tract of land I now live on I purchased of Mr. TRAVERSE WAUGH .. if he dies without heirs to his Brother, SAMUEL BAYLY .. to my daughter, NANCY BAYLY, the warehouses and lotts thereunto belonging also the lotts whereon my wife lived and died in Town of Colchester .. if she dies without heirs to my son, PIERCE BAYLY .. to my grandson, ROBERT BOGGESS, that land I purchased of SAMUEL BAYLY in Fauquier containing by estimation 180 acres when he arrives to the age of twenty one years .. if he dies without heirs to my granddaughter, BETTY BOGGESS .. desire my Executors give said BETTY BOGGESS One hundred pounds lawful money .. also One hundred pounds to my granddaughter, NANCY, who married JOHN SINGLETON. I give my Cousin, MOLLY WILLSON, my old black mare or colt whichever she chooses .. there are three or four tracts of land I have not mentioned which I desire may be equally divided among my seven sons, there is my Mill Tract & WILLIAM EATON

and ROBERT WHITLEY Tract lying on popeshead which I desire may be divided equally according to quantity and quality between my sons, PIERCE BAYLY, WILLIAM BAYLY, SAMUEL BAYLY, JOSEPH BAYLY, MOUNTJOY BAYLY, TAPLY BAYLY and ROBERT BAYLY .. appoint PIERCE BAYLY, WILLIAM BAYLY and SAMUEL BAYLY Executors .. this 25th day of July 1781.
Witness W. Thompson,
Ay. Labat Wm. Bayly

At a court held .. xxth May 1782 .. will proved by ANTHONY LABAT and at a court held .. 16th September in year afsd will proved by (Executors named) .. admitted to record .. certificate is granted them for obtaining a probate thereof ..

pp. 441-445 Will of WILLIAM PAYNE. I WILLIAM PAYNE of Parish of Fairfax in the county of Fairfax being in perfect Sence & memory .. give unto my son, WILLIAM PAYNE, 150 acres of land to be laid off of the land I bought of JOSIAH WATSON .. likewise give him half my Leese to live on said plantation and if he shall think proper to leave it and remove away, the whole of the said Leese to my son, DEVAUL PAYNE. I give my son, WILLIAM PAYNE, four negroes .. Fan is in possession of COLO. CHARLES BROADWATER. I give to my loving son, BENJAMIN CLARKE PAYNE, my Leese where (he) now lives, also my Leese where WILLIAM GOODING lives, also my Mill Seat on Accotink run .. also four negroes .. Cate in possession of Colo. CHARLES BROADWATER .. I give to my loving son, DEVAUL PAYNE, the remainder part of that parcel of land I bought of JOSIAH WATSON after laying off 150 acres (given son, WILLIAM) .. likewise my Leese for the plantation where I now live in case his Brother, WILLIAM PAYNE, shall choose to remove away .. if he (DEVAUL) dies without heirs then his part to be equally divided between his Brothers & Sistars, Vizt. WILLIAM PAYNE, BENJAMIN CLARKE PAYNE, ALICIA COOKE, MARY BALLEY, PENELAPHA PAYNE, ANN WEST .. to my loving daughter, ALICIA COOKE, three negroes .. to my loving daughter, MARY BALEY, three negroes .. Charles is in possession of CHARLES BROADWATER .. also give my granddaughter, ANNE BALEY, one cow and calf to the care of her father, PIERCE BAYLY .. to my loving daughter, ANN WEST, three negroes .. give my loving daughter, PENALAPHA PAYNE, three negroes .. give my half sister, MILLY PAYNE, one cow and calf to be taken care of by her Brother, JOHN PAYNE, till she marrys or comes with age. It is my desire that my land warrants for ten thousand acres in the back inhabitance to be put in the hands of some person to be located then to be equally divided among such of my children as will be willing to pay their way their equal proportion of their Expence .. remainder of my Estate to be sold .. and equally divided among my seven children, Vizt. WILLIAM PAYNE, BENJAMIN CLARKE PAYNE, DEVAUL PAYNE, ALICIA COOKE, MARY BALY, PENELAPHA PAYNE and ANNA WEST .. appoint my three sons, WILLIAM PAYNE, BENJAMIN CLARKE PAYNE & DEVAUL PAYNE, Executors .. this 27th day May 1782.

Presence Samson Cockerill, W. Payne
William Tasker, James Richards,
Thos. Fitzhugh, John Payne

At a court held .. xxth August 1782 .. will presented by WILLIAM PAYNE & BENJAMIN CLARK PAYNE .. admitted to record .. certificate is granted them for obtaining a probate thereof ..

End of Fairfax County Will Book D

P. Wagener Cl Cur

Page

73 BALENDINE, John
57 BALLENGER, William
86 BALSOR. Gasper
63 BAYLISS, Thomas
87 BAYLY. William
80 BEALL, Sophia
60 BEELER, Christopher
85 BLATT, John
64 BOWLING. Gerrard
17 BOWMAKER, James
84 BROWN, Gracie
76 BUCHANAN, Elizabeth

67 CARLYLE, John
25 CARSON, Thomas
71 CHAPIN, Benjamin
39 CHEW, Mercy
35 CLARK, John
36 CLIFTON, Elizabeth
75 COFFER, Daniel Withers
79 COLELOUGH, Benjamin
24 COLVILL, Frances
46 CONNILL, James
38 CORNISH, Charles
42 CORNISH, Elizabeth
34 COYLE, Michael
18 CROSSWAIT, Anthony

71 DADE, Townshend
47 DALTON, John
45 DARRELL, Augustus
18 DARRELL, George
51 DARRELL, Sampson
18 DOGIN, John
15 DONALDSON, James
85 DORRELL, Cordelia
17 DOWDALL, Thomas
78 DULIN, Edward

13 FARGUSON, Joshua
43 FORD, Thomas
22 FRENCH, Daniel
8 FRIZEL, William

56 GARRET, William
44 GOARD, Mary
37 GOSSOM, William

59 HALLEYS, Samuel
72 HARDEN, William
76 HARPER, Robert
46 HAWKINS, Mary
63 HOUGH, Lawrence
44 HUNTER, George

28 JOHNSON, Samuel
20 JOHNSTON, Hannah
13 JOHNSTON, Mary
10 JOHNSTON, Samuel

31 KENT, Benoni
19 KENT, Richard

35 LAKE, Richard
12 LAMPHIER, Venus
85 LANGMARCH, Christian
39 LESTER, William
20 LEWIS, Thomas

10 McINTOSH, John
33 MANLEY, Harrison
62 MASON, Philip
2 MILLS, Alexander
63 MINOR, John
24 MOORE, Henry
11 MOORE, William
54 MOSS, Thomas
66 MUIR, James
86 MUNDAY, William

56 PATTERSON, Fleming
6 PATTERSON, John
42 PAYNE, William
88 PAYNE, William
64 PIPER, Harry

29 REAGAN, Michael
22 RIGDON, Edward
78 ROBERTSON, George
8 ROBERTSON, James Senr.
86 RUMNEY, William

12 SANFORD, Robert
16 SEBASTIAN, Benjamin Senr
33 SEBASTIAN, Elizabeth
7 SHAW, Jane
50 SHAW, Thomas
35 SHAW, William
5 SHERIDON, John
4 SIMONS, Ann
77 SIMPSON, George
29 SIMPSON, Gilbert
40 SMITH, Margery
58 SPINKS, John
52 STEUART, Andrew
72 STEUART, James

47 TAYLOR, Thomas
27 THOM, William
7 THOMAS, Robert
9 TURLEY, Jane
34 TURLEY, Paul
51 TURLEY, Paul

25 VILET, Edward
16 VILET, Ewel

1 WEST, Hugh
49 WEST, John
45 WEST, John Junr.
76 WICKLIFF, Robert
43 WILLIAMS, John
38 WILLIAMS, Owen
39 WISHEART, Henry
5 WREN, Thomas

55 ZUILL, Robert

Heritage Books by Ruth and Sam Sparacio

Abstracts of Account Books of Edward Dixon, Merchant of Port Royal, Virginia, Volume I: 1743–1747

Abstracts of Account Books of Edward Dixon, Merchant of Port Royal, Virginia, Volume II

Albemarle County, Virginia Deed and Will Book Abstracts, 1748–1752

Albemarle County, Virginia Deed Book Abstracts, 1758–1761

Albemarle County, Virginia Deed Book Abstracts, 1761–1764

Albemarle County, Virginia Deed Book Abstracts, 1764–1768

Albemarle County, Virginia Deed Book Abstracts, 1768–1770

Albemarle County, Virginia Deed Book Abstracts, 1771–1772

Albemarle County, Virginia Deed Book Abstracts, 1772–1776

Albemarle County, Virginia Deed Book Abstracts, 1776–1778

Albemarle County, Virginia Deed Book Abstracts, 1778–1780

Albemarle County, Virginia Deed Book Abstracts, 1780–1783

Albemarle County, Virginia Deed Book Abstracts, 1783–1785

Albemarle County, Virginia Deed Book Abstracts, 1785–1787

Albemarle County, Virginia Deed Book Abstracts, 1787–1790

Albemarle County, Virginia Deed Book Abstracts, 1790–1791

Albemarle County, Virginia Deed Book Abstracts, 1791–1793

Albemarle County, Virginia Deed Book Abstracts, 1793–1794

Albemarle County, Virginia Deed Book Abstracts, 1794–1795

Albemarle County, Virginia Deed Book Abstracts, 1795–1796

Albemarle County, Virginia Deed Book Abstracts, 1796–1797

Albemarle County, Virginia Will Book Abstracts: 1752–1756 and 1775–1783

Albemarle County, Virginia Will Book: 2, 1752–1764

Albemarle County, Virginia Wills, 1764–1775

Albemarle County, Virginia Will Book: 3, 1785–1798

Augusta County, Virginia Land Tax Books, 1782–1788

Augusta County, Virginia Land Tax Books, 1788–1790

Amherst County, Virginia Land Tax Books, 1789–1791

Caroline County, Virginia Appeals and Land Causes, 1787–1794

Caroline County, Virginia Appeals and Land Causes, 1795–1800

Caroline County, Virginia Committee of Safety and Early Surveys, 1729–1762 and 1774–1775

Caroline County, Virginia Guardian Bonds 1806–1821

Caroline County, Virginia Land Tax Book Alterations, 1782–1789

Caroline County, Virginia Land Tax Book Alterations, 1789–1792

Caroline County, Virginia Land Tax Book Alterations, 1792–1795

Caroline County, Virginia Land Tax Book Alterations, 1795–1798

Caroline County, Virginia Order Book Abstracts, 1765

Caroline County, Virginia Order Book Abstracts, 1767–1768

Caroline County, Virginia Order Book Abstracts, 1768–1770

Caroline County, Virginia Order Book Abstracts, 1770–1771

Caroline County, Virginia Order Book, 1764

Caroline County, Virginia Order Book, 1765–1767

Caroline County, Virginia Order Book, 1771–1772

Caroline County, Virginia Order Book, 1772–1773

Caroline County, Virginia Order Book, 1773

Caroline County, Virginia Order Book, 1773–1774

Caroline County, Virginia Order Book, 1774–1778

Caroline County, Virginia Order Book, 1778–1781

Caroline County, Virginia Order Book, 1781–1783

Caroline County, Virginia Order Book, 1783–1784

Caroline County, Virginia Order Book, 1784–1785

Caroline County, Virginia Order Book, 1785–1786

Caroline County, Virginia Order Book, 1786–1787

Caroline County, Virginia Order Book, 1787, Part 1

Caroline County, Virginia Order Book, 1787, Part 2

Caroline County, Virginia Order Book, 1787–1788

Caroline County, Virginia Order Book, 1788

Culpeper County, Virginia Deed Book Abstracts, 1769–1773

Culpeper County, Virginia Deed Book Abstracts,1778–1779

Culpeper County, Virginia Deed Book Abstracts, 1781–1783

Culpeper County, Virginia Deed Book Abstracts, 1785–1786

Culpeper County, Virginia Deed Book Abstracts,1788–1789

Culpeper County, Virginia Deed Book Abstracts, 1791–1792

Culpeper County, Virginia Deed Book Abstracts, 1795–1796

Culpeper County, Virginia Land Tax Book, 1782–1786

Culpeper County, Virginia Land Tax Book, 1787–1789

Culpeper County, Virginia Minute Book, 1763–1764

Digest of Family Relationships, 1650–1692, from Virginia County Court Records

Digest of Family Relationships, 1720–1750, from Virginia County Court Records

Digest of Family Relationships, 1750–1763, from Virginia County Court Records

Digest of Family Relationships, 1764–1775, from Virginia County Court Records

Essex County, Virginia Deed and Will Abstracts, 1695–1697

Essex County, Virginia Deed and Will Abstracts, 1697–1699

Essex County, Virginia Deed and Will Abstracts, 1699–1701

Essex County, Virginia Deed and Will Abstracts, 1701–1703

Essex County, Virginia Deed and Will Book, 1692–1693

Essex County, Virginia Deed and Will Book, 1693–1694

Essex County, Virginia Deed and Will Book, 1694–1695

Essex County, Virginia Deed and Will Book, 1695–1697

Essex County, Virginia Deed and Will Book, 1697–1699

Essex County, Virginia Deed and Will Book, 1701–1704

Essex County, Virginia Deed and Will Book, 1745–1749

Essex County, Virginia Deed, 1753–1754 and Will Book 1750

Essex County, Virginia Deed Abstracts, 1721–1724

Essex County, Virginia Deed Book, 1724–1728

Essex County, Virginia Deed Book, 1728–1733

Essex County, Virginia Deed Book, 1733–1738

Essex County, Virginia Deed Book, 1738–1742

Essex County, Virginia Deed Book, 1742–1745

Essex County, Virginia Deed Abstracts, 1745–1749

Essex County, Virginia Deed Book, 1749–1751

Essex County, Virginia Deed Book, 1751–1753

Essex County, Virginia Land Trials Abstracts, 1711–1741

Essex County, Virginia Order Book Abstracts, 1695–1699

Essex County, Virginia Order Book Abstracts, 1699–1702

Essex County, Virginia Order Book Abstracts, 1716–1723, Part 1

Essex County, Virginia Order Book Abstracts, 1716–1723, Part 2

Essex County, Virginia Order Book Abstracts, 1716–1723, Part 3
Essex County, Virginia Order Book Abstracts, 1716–1723, Part 4
Essex County, Virginia Order Book Abstracts, 1723–1725, Part 1
Essex County, Virginia Order Book Abstracts, 1723–1725, Part 2
Essex County, Virginia Order Book Abstracts, 1725–1729, Part 1
Essex County, Virginia Order Book Abstracts, 1727–1729, Part 2
Essex County, Virginia Order Book, 1695–1699
Essex County, Virginia Will Abstracts, 1730–1735
Essex County, Virginia Will Abstracts, 1735–1743
Essex County, Virginia Will Abstracts, 1743–1744
Essex County, Virginia Will Abstracts, 1745–1748
Essex County, Virginia Will Abstracts, 1748–1750
Fairfax County, Virginia Deed Abstracts, 1799–1800 and 1803–1804
Fairfax County, Virginia Deed Abstracts, 1804–1805
Fairfax County, Virginia Deed Book, 1795–1796
Fairfax County, Virginia Deed Book, 1796–1797
Fairfax County, Virginia Deed Book Abstracts, 1774–1777
Fairfax County, Virginia Deed Book Abstracts, 1788–1789
Fairfax County, Virginia Deed Book Abstracts, 1789–1791
Fairfax County, Virginia Deed Book Abstracts, 1796
Fairfax County, Virginia Deed Book Abstracts, 1799
Fairfax County, Virginia Deed Book Abstracts, 1783–1784
Fairfax County, Virginia Deed Book Abstracts, 1785–1788
Fairfax County, Virginia Deed Book, 1798–1799
Fairfax County, Virginia Index and References to Missing Deed Book N, 1778–1783
Fairfax County, Virginia Land Causes, 1788–1824
Fairfax County, Virginia Order Book Abstracts, 1768–1769
Fairfax County, Virginia Order Book Abstracts, 1769–1770
Fairfax County, Virginia Will Book Abstracts, 1742–1745
Fairfax County, Virginia Will Book Abstracts, 1745–1748
Fairfax County, Virginia Will Book Abstracts, 1767–1783
Fauquier County, Virginia Land Tax Book, 1783–1787
Fauquier County, Virginia Land Tax Book, 1787–1791
Fauquier County, Virginia Minute Book Abstracts, 1759–1761
Fauquier County, Virginia Minute Book Abstracts, 1761–1762
Fauquier County, Virginia Minute Book Abstracts, 1762–1763
Fauquier County, Virginia Minute Book Abstracts, 1763–1764
Fauquier County, Virginia Minute Book Abstracts, 1764–1766
Fauquier County, Virginia Minute Book Abstracts, 1766–1767
Fauquier County, Virginia Minute Book Abstracts, 1767–1769
Fauquier County, Virginia Minute Book Abstracts, 1769–1771
Fauquier County, Virginia Minute Book Abstracts, 1771–1772
Fauquier County, Virginia Minute Book Abstracts, 1772–1773
Fauquier County, Virginia Minute Book Abstracts, 1773–1775
Fauquier County, Virginia Minute Book Abstracts, 1775–1779
Fauquier County, Virginia Minute Book Abstracts, 1779–1782
Fauquier County, Virginia Minute Book Abstracts, 1782–1783
Fauquier County, Virginia Minute Book Abstracts, 1783–1784
Fauquier County, Virginia Minute Book Abstracts, 1784–1785
Fauquier County, Virginia Minute Book Abstracts, 1785–1786
Fauquier County, Virginia Minute Book Abstracts, 1786–1787
Fauquier County, Virginia Minute Book Abstracts, 1787
Fauquier County, Virginia Minute Book Abstracts, 1787–1788
Fauquier County, Virginia Minute Book Abstracts, 1788–1789
Fauquier County, Virginia Minute Book Abstracts, 1789–1790
Fredericksburg City, Virginia Deed Book, 1782–1787
Fredericksburg City, Virginia Deed Book, 1787–1794
Fredericksburg City, Virginia Deed Book, 1794–1804
Hanover County, Virginia Land Tax Book, 1782–1788
Hanover County, Virginia Land Tax Book, 1789–1793
Hanover County, Virginia Land Tax Book, 1793–1796
King George County, Virginia Deed Book Abstracts, 1721–1735
King George County, Virginia Deed Book Abstracts, 1735–1752
King George County, Virginia Deed Book Abstracts, 1753–1773
King George County, Virginia Deed Book Abstracts, 1773–1783
King George County, Virginia Deed Book Abstracts, 1787–1790
King George County, Virginia Deed Book Abstracts, 1773–1783
King George County, Virginia Deed Book Abstracts, 1780–1787
King George County, Virginia Deed Book Abstracts, 1792–1794
King George County, Virginia Inventories, 1745–1765
King George County, Virginia Order Book Abstracts, 1721–1723
King George County, Virginia Order Book Abstracts, 1725–1728
King George County, Virginia Will Book Abstracts, 1752–1780
King William County, Virginia Record Book, 1702–1705
King William County, Virginia Record Book, 1705–1721
King William County, Virginia Record Book, 1722 and 1785–1786
Lancaster County, Virginia Deed and Will Book, 1652–1657
Lancaster County, Virginia Deed and Will Book, 1654–1661
Lancaster County, Virginia Deed and Will Book, 1661–1702 (1661–1666 and 1699–1702)
Lancaster County, Virginia Deed Book Abstracts, 1701–1706
Lancaster County, Virginia Deed Book, 1706–1710
Lancaster County, Virginia Deed Book, 1710–1714
Lancaster County, Virginia Order Book Abstracts, 1656–1661
Lancaster County, Virginia Order Book Abstracts, 1662–1666
Lancaster County, Virginia Order Book Abstracts, 1666–1669
Lancaster County, Virginia Order Book Abstracts, 1670–1674
Lancaster County, Virginia Order Book Abstracts, 1674–1678
Lancaster County, Virginia Order Book Abstracts, 1678–1681
Lancaster County, Virginia Order Book Abstracts, 1682–1687
Lancaster County, Virginia Order Book Abstracts, 1691–1695
Lancaster County, Virginia Order Book Abstracts, 1729–1732
Lancaster County, Virginia Order Book Abstracts, 1736–1739
Lancaster County, Virginia Order Book Abstracts, 1739–1742
Lancaster County, Virginia Order Book, 1687–1691
Lancaster County, Virginia Order Book, 1691–1695
Lancaster County, Virginia Order Book, 1695–1699
Lancaster County, Virginia Order Book, 1699–1701
Lancaster County, Virginia Order Book, 1701–1703
Lancaster County, Virginia Order Book, 1703–1706
Lancaster County, Virginia Order Book, 1732–1736
Lancaster County, Virginia Will Book, 1675–1689
Lancaster County, Virginia Will Book, 1690–1709
Loudoun County, Virginia Order Book, 1757–1758
Loudoun County, Virginia Order Book, 1763–1764
Loudoun County, Virginia Order Book, 1764
Louisa County, Virginia Deed Book Abstracts, 1742–1744

Louisa County, Virginia Deed Book Abstracts, 1744–1746

Louisa County, Virginia Order Book, 1742–1744

Louisa County, Virginia, Orders, 1744–1747

Louisa County, Virginia Orders 1747–1748, 1766, and 1772

Louisa County, Virginia, Orders, 1772–1774

Louisa County, Virginia, Order Book Abstracts, 1767–1768

Louisa County, Virginia, Orders, 1769–1770

Louisa County, Virginia, Orders, 1770–1772

Louisa County, Virginia, Orders, 1772–1774

Madison County, Virginia Deed Book Abstracts, 1793–1804

Madison County, Virginia Deed Book, 1793–1813, and Marriage Bonds, 1793–1800

Middlesex County, Virginia Deed Book Abstracts, 1679–1688

Middlesex County, Virginia Deed Book Abstracts, 1688–1694

Middlesex County, Virginia Deed Book Abstracts, 1694–1703

Middlesex County, Virginia Deed Book Abstracts, 1703–1709

Middlesex County, Virginia Deed Book Abstracts, 1709–1720

Middlesex County, Virginia Order Book Abstracts, 1680–1686

Middlesex County, Virginia Order Book Abstracts, 1686–1690

Middlesex County, Virginia Order Book Abstracts, 1697–1700

Middlesex County, Virginia Order Book Abstracts, 1700–1702

Middlesex County, Virginia Order Book Abstracts, 1705–1707

Middlesex County, Virginia Order Book Abstracts, 1707–1708

Middlesex County, Virginia Order Book Abstracts, 1708–1710

Middlesex County, Virginia Order Book Abstracts, 1710–1712

Middlesex County, Virginia Order Book Abstracts, 1712–1714

Middlesex County, Virginia Order Book Abstracts, 1714–1716

Middlesex County, Virginia Order Book Abstracts, 1716–1719

Middlesex County, Virginia Order Book Abstracts, 1719–1721

Middlesex County, Virginia Order Book Abstracts, 1721–1724

Middlesex County, Virginia Order Book Abstracts, 1732–1737

Middlesex County, Virginia Order Book Abstracts, 1740–1745

Middlesex County, Virginia Record Book Abstracts, 1721–1813

Northumberland County, Virginia Deed and Will Book, 1650–1655

Northumberland County, Virginia Deed and Will Book, 1655–1658

Northumberland County, Virginia Deed and Will Book, 1658–1662

Northumberland County, Virginia Deed and Will Book, 1662–1666

Northumberland County, Virginia Deed and Will Book, 1666–1670

Northumberland County, Virginia Deed and Will Book, 1670–1672 and 1706–1711

Northumberland County, Virginia Deed and Will Book, 1711–1712

Northumberland County, Virginia Deed and Will Book, 1712–1726

Northumberland County, Virginia Order Book, 1652–1657

Northumberland County, Virginia Order Book, 1657–1661

Northumberland County, Virginia Order Book, 1661–1665

Northumberland County, Virginia Order Book, 1665–1669

Northumberland County, Virginia Order Book, 1669–1673

Northumberland County, Virginia Order Book, 1674–1677

Northumberland County, Virginia Order Book, 1677–1679

Northumberland County, Virginia Order Book, 1680–1683

Northumberland County, Virginia Order Book, 1683–1686

Northumberland County, Virginia Order Book, 1699–1700

Northumberland County, Virginia Order Book, 1700–1702

Northumberland County, Virginia Order Book, 1702–1704

Orange County, Virginia, Chancery Suits, 1831–1845

Orange County, Virginia Deeds, 1743–1759

Orange County, Virginia Deed Book Abstracts, 1759–1778

Orange County, Virginia Deed Book Abstracts, 1778–1786

Orange County, Virginia Deed Book Abstracts, 1795–1797

Orange County, Virginia Deed Book Abstracts, 1797–1799

Orange County, Virginia Deed Book Abstracts, 1799–1800

Orange County, Virginia Deed Book Abstracts, 1800–1802

Orange County, Virginia Deed Book Abstracts, 1786–1791, Deed Book 19

Orange County, Virginia Deed Book Abstracts, 1791–1795, Deed Book 20

Orange County, Virginia Deed Book Abstracts, 1795–1797, Deed Book 21

Orange County, Virginia, Digest of Will Abstracts, 1734–1838

Orange County, Virginia Land Tax Book, 1782–1790

Orange County, Virginia Land Tax Book, 1791–1795

Orange County, Virginia Order Book Abstracts, 1747–1748

Orange County, Virginia Order Book Abstracts, 1748–1749

Orange County, Virginia Order Book Abstracts, 1749–1752

Orange County, Virginia Order Book Abstracts, 1752–1753

Orange County, Virginia Order Book Abstracts, 1753–1754

Orange County, Virginia Order Book Abstracts, 1755–1756

Orange County, Virginia Order Book Abstracts, 1756–1757

Orange County, Virginia Order Book Abstracts, 1757–1759

Orange County, Virginia Order Book Abstracts, 1759–1762

Orange County, Virginia Order Book Abstracts, 1762–1763

Orange County, Virginia Will Abstracts, 1778–1821

Orange County, Virginia Will Abstracts, 1821–1838

Orange County, Virginia, Will Digest, 1734–1838

Pamunkey Neighbors of Orange County, Virginia (Transcriptions from the original files of County Courts in Virginia, Kentucky and Missouri of wills, deeds, order books & marriages as well as some family lines...)

A Supplement to Pamunkey Neighbors of Orange County, Virginia, Volumes 1 and 2

Ruth and Sam Sparacio, Luretta and Eldon Corkill

Petersburg City, Virginia Hustings Court Deed Book Abstracts: 1784–1787 1787–1790 1790–1793

Prince William County, Virginia Court Orders 1763 and 1766–1767

Prince William County, Virginia Deed Book Abstracts, 1740–1741

Prince William County, Virginia Deed Book Abstracts, 1745–1746 and 1748–1749

Prince William County, Virginia Deed Book Abstracts, 1749–1752

Prince William County, Virginia Deed Abstracts, 1749–1752 and 1761–1764

Prince William County, Virginia Deed Book Abstracts, 1763–1768

Prince William County, Virginia Deed Book Abstracts, 1767–1771

Prince William County, Virginia Deed Book Abstracts, 1774–1779

Prince William County, Virginia Deed Book Abstracts, 1779–1784

Prince William County, Virginia Deed Book Abstracts, 1784–1787

Prince William County, Virginia Deed Book Abstracts, 1787–1791

Prince William County, Virginia Deed Book Abstracts, 1791–1794

Prince William County, Virginia Deed Book Abstracts, 1794–1796

Prince William County, Virginia Deed Book Abstracts, 1796–1798

Prince William County, Virginia Deed Book Abstracts, 1798–1799

Prince William County, Virginia District Court Orders, 1793 (Part 1)

Prince William County, Virginia Land Causes Abstracts, 1789–1790
Prince William County, Virginia Land Causes Abstracts, 1790–1793
Prince William County, Virginia Order Book Abstracts, 1752–1753
Prince William County, Virginia Order Book Abstracts, 1753–1757
Prince William County, Virginia Order Book 1762
Prince William County, Virginia Order Book, 1762–1763
Prince William County, Virginia District Court Orders, 1793 (Part 2)
(Old) Rappahannock County, Virginia Deed Book Abstracts, 1682–1686
(Old) Rappahannock County, Virginia Deed and Will Book Abstracts:
1656–1662 1662–1665 1663–1668 1665–1677
1668–1670 1670–1672 1672–1673/4 1673/4–1676
1677–1678/9 1678/9–1682 1682–1686 1686–1688
1688–1692
(Old) Rappahannock County, Virginia Order Book Abstracts, 1683–1685
(Old) Rappahannock County, Virginia Order Book Abstracts, 1685–1687
(Old) Rappahannock County, Virginia Order Book Abstracts, 1687–1689
(Old) Rappahannock County, Virginia Order Book Abstracts, 1689–1692
(Old) Rappahannock County, Virginia Will Book Abstracts, 1682–1687
Richmond City, Virginia Hustings Deed Book, 1782–1790
Richmond City, Virginia Hustings Deed Book, 1790–1794
Richmond County, Virginia Account Book Abstracts, 1724–1751
Richmond County, Virginia Account Book Abstracts, 1751–1783
Richmond County, Virginia Deed Book Abstracts, 1692–1695
Richmond County, Virginia Deed Book Abstracts, 1695–1701
Richmond County, Virginia Deed Book Abstracts, 1701–1704
Richmond County, Virginia Deed Book Abstracts, 1705–1708
Richmond County, Virginia Deed Book Abstracts, 1708–1711
Richmond County, Virginia Deed Book Abstracts, 1711–1714
Richmond County, Virginia Deed Book Abstracts, 1715–1718
Richmond County, Virginia Deed Book Abstracts, 1718–1719
Richmond County, Virginia Deed Book Abstracts, 1719–1721
Richmond County, Virginia Deed Book Abstracts, 1721–1725
Richmond County, Virginia Order Book Abstracts, 1692–1694
Richmond County, Virginia Order Book Abstracts, 1694–1697
Richmond County, Virginia Order Book Abstracts, 1697–1699
Richmond County, Virginia Order Book Abstracts, 1699–1701
Richmond County, Virginia Order Book Abstracts, 1702–1704
Richmond County, Virginia Order Book Abstracts, 1704–1705
Richmond County, Virginia Order Book Abstracts, 1705–1706
Richmond County, Virginia Order Book Abstracts, 1707–1708
Richmond County, Virginia Order Book Abstracts, 1708–1709
Richmond County, Virginia Order Book Abstracts, 1709–1710
Richmond County, Virginia Order Book Abstracts, 1710–1711
Richmond County, Virginia Order Book Abstracts, 1711–1713
Richmond County, Virginia Order Book Abstracts, 1714–1715
Richmond County, Virginia Order Book Abstracts, 1715–1716
Richmond County, Virginia Order Book Abstracts, 1716–1717
Richmond County, Virginia Order Book Abstracts, 1717–1718
Richmond County, Virginia Order Book Abstracts, 1718–1719
Richmond County, Virginia Order Book Abstracts, 1719–1721
Richmond County, Virginia Order Book Abstracts, 1721–1725
Richmond County, Virginia Order Book Abstracts, 1737–1738
Richmond County, Virginia Order Book Abstracts, 1738–1740
Spotsylvania County, Virginia Deed Book, 1722–1725
Spotsylvania County, Virginia Deed Book, 1725–1728
Spotsylvania County, Virginia Deed Book, 1728–1729
Spotsylvania County, Virginia Deed Book, 1729–1730
Spotsylvania County, Virginia Deed Book: 1730–1731
Spotsylvania County, Virginia Order Book Abstracts:
1724–1730 (Part I: Sept. 1724–Nov. 1726)
Spotsylvania County, Virginia Order Book Abstracts:
1724–1730 (Part II) and *1724–1730 (Part III)*
Spotsylvania County, Virginia Order Book Abstracts, 1730–1732
Spotsylvania County, Virginia Order Book Abstracts, 1732–1734
Spotsylvania County, Virginia Order Book Abstracts, 1734–1735
Spotsylvania County, Virginia Order Book Abstracts, 1735–1738
Spotsylvania County, Virginia Order Book Abstracts, 1738–1740
Spotsylvania County, Virginia Order Book Abstracts, 1740–1742
Spotsylvania County, Virginia Order Book Abstracts, 1742–1744
Spotsylvania County, Virginia Order Book Abstracts, 1744–1746
Spotsylvania County, Virginia Order Book Abstracts, 1746–1748
Spotsylvania County, Virginia Order Book Abstracts, 1749–1751
Stafford County, Virginia Deed and Will Book, 1686–1689
Stafford County, Virginia Deed and Will Book, 1689–1693
Stafford County, Virginia Deed and Will Book, 1699–1709
Stafford County, Virginia Deed and Will Book, 1780–1786,
and Scheme Book Orders, 1790–1793
Stafford County, Virginia Deed and Will Abstracts, 1810–1813
Stafford County, Virginia Deed and Will Abstracts, 1825–1826
Stafford County, Virginia Deed and Will Book Abstracts,
1785–1786 and 1809–1810
Stafford County, Virginia Deed Book, 1722–1728 and 1755–1765
Stafford County, Virginia Land Tax Books, 1782–1792
Stafford County, Virginia Order Book, 1664–1668 and 1689–1690
Stafford County, Virginia Order Book, 1691–1692
Stafford County, Virginia Order Book, 1692–1693
Stafford County, Virginia Will Book, 1729–1748
Stafford County, Virginia Will Book, 1748–1767
Westmoreland County, Virginia Deed and Will Abstracts, 1723–1726
Westmoreland County, Virginia Deed and Will Abstracts, 1726–1729
Westmoreland County, Virginia Deed and Will Abstracts, 1729–1732
Westmoreland County, Virginia Deed and Will Abstracts, 1732–1734
Westmoreland County, Virginia Deed and Will Abstracts, 1734–1736
Westmoreland County, Virginia Deed and Will Abstracts, 1736–1740
Westmoreland County, Virginia Deed and Will Abstracts, 1740–1742
Westmoreland County, Virginia Deed and Will Abstracts, 1742–1745
Westmoreland County, Virginia Deed and Will Abstracts, 1745–1747
Westmoreland County, Virginia Deed and Will Abstracts, 1747–1748
Westmoreland County, Virginia Deed and Will Abstracts, 1749–1751
Westmoreland County, Virginia Deed and Will Abstracts, 1751–1754
Westmoreland County, Virginia Deed and Will Abstracts, 1754–1756
Westmoreland County, Virginia Order Book, 1705–1707
Westmoreland County, Virginia Order Book, 1707–1709
Westmoreland County, Virginia Order Book, 1709–1712
Westmoreland County, Virginia Order Book, 1712–1714
Westmoreland County, Virginia Order Book, 1714–1716
Westmoreland County, Virginia Order Book, 1716–1718
Westmoreland County, Virginia Order Book, 1718–1721

www.ingramcontent.com/pod-product-compliance
Lightning Source LLC
LaVergne TN
LVHW061251100826
845148LV00008B/1089
9781680345490